JAZZTALK

JAZZTALK

The *Cadence* Interviews
by Robert D. Rusch

Lyle Stuart Inc. *Secaucus, New Jersey*

Library of Congress Cataloging in Publication Data

Library of Congress Cataloging in Publication Data

Rusch, Robert D.
JazzTalk.

Includes index.
1. Jazz musicians—United States—Interviews.
I. Title.
ML395.R87 1984 785.42'092'2 [B] 83-18065
ISBN 0-8184-0357-8

Published by Lyle Stuart Inc.
Published simultaneously in Canada by
Musson Book Company,
A division of General Publishing Co. Limited
Don Mills, Ontario

Queries regarding rights and permissions should be addressed to: Lyle Stuart, 120 Enterprise Avenue, Secaucus, N.J. 07094

Manufactured in the United States of America

To Joe "King" Oliver, whom I have always wanted to do an oral history with, and to all the other masters of music who have passed before us undocumented by their own oral history.

ACKNOWLEDGMENTS

This work could not have happened without the dedicated and selfless efforts of its author. However, those efforts would have been impossible without interplay with, among others, my mother who encouraged my interest in creative improvised music, and my father, who unwittingly gave me support in my pursuance of that interest; Tom Lord, an angel; the musicians involved, for their participation in these interviews; Kathy Joyce for support; R.J. for his consultation; Marc Rusch, Kea Rusch, Kara Rusch, Robin Rusch, and Susan Rusch whose cooperation and communal spirit continue to make possible the turning of dreams into realities.

Contents

Introduction

My first interview was in 1956 with W.C. Handy in his home at Tuckahoe, New York. Raised on a diet of Vivaldi, Bach, Beethoven, and other music from the Baroque and Classic periods of European music, I had become attracted to the equally hip creations of my *other brothers*. And as a teenager I was already seasoned in Armstrong, Waller, Goodman, Ellington, Hampton, Krupa, Parker and Brubeck. Bach or Bird, it was all music which moved me and rewarded the efforts demanded of its listener.

I guess one of the basics of this music called Jazz was W.C. Handy. I knew him through the Blues—Yellow Dog, Hesitating, Atlanta, Memphis, Beale Street, Aunt Hagar's and St. Louis. I would have liked to have spoken to Bach or Vivaldi, to have heard them speak of their music and tried to understand through language what brings about a *Mass in B Minor* or *The Four Seasons*. So when I found out W.C. Handy was alive and living within traveling distance, I arranged to travel to Tuckahoe to interview him. I took with me a school friend (also attuned to Jazz), and his father's Dictaphone, which cut green floppy discs and weighed what seemed like 100 pounds.

Mr. Handy came down the stairs on a chair elevator. Wide-eyed and hanging onto his every word, we talked to him and he transported us back to those arcane Southern experiences of recent ancient history—those pre-Armstrong days which helped formulate this wondrous music. Mr. Handy talked, sang, and even cried, and I don't think I ever took my eyes off his face as I tried to fix forever the uniqueness of the moment.

By this time in his life, Mr. Handy was blind, and in our enthusiasm we held the mike only a few inches from his mouth. Unfortunately, this made the recording so distorted that we could make very little out of it. Years later I tried to trace down the little green discs but it seems that they had been discarded. My most lasting memory of what Mr. Handy had to say that day was his answer to our inquiry about how he developed his lyrics. He simply said that he really didn't create the lyrics but more or less adapted the music from the talk that he heard: "For instance, you might pass by a back lot where two women might be out hanging laundry or speaking to each other across a fence and one might say, 'Whew, *If I'm feeling tomorrow as bad as I do today I'm going to go away.*' I just rearrange what I might hear."

His lack of pretense was both disarming and revealing. It made his Blues seem no less magnificent, but at the same time made them come vividly to life. Since then I have not only been hooked on the music, but also on the oral history of the makers of the music.

Interviews are rather similar to improvisations. A good improviser uses just enough familiar materials (clichés, if you will) to give the listener bearings and, with these, creates strong original statements. These statements move the listener with their searching, mobility, and revelation.

Interviews with creative improvising artists demonstrate both the similarity of their situations and the individuality of each artist's experiences and reactions to them. These are very special people, people who, in spite of their very difficult existence, often devote the greater part of their lives and energy to creating communications by sound that possess extraordinary power and beauty. These are positive constructive acts which for the most part go unrecognized by a society with other priorities, but which nevertheless can often be found to have had influences in the genesis of much of the Western World's culture of the 20th century.

Since W.C. Handy, I have interviewed and listened to the oral histories of hundreds of Jazz and Blues artists. In 1976, I began in the pages of *Cadence Magazine* to document more formally these encounters. *Cadence Magazine* was established mainly to serve two great needs. One was the documentation, with discography and comment, of a good portion of the thousands of records being released each year by creative improvising artists. Thus during its first eight years *Cadence Magazine* reviewed over 10,000 different Jazz and Blues releases from all over the world. The other objective was to begin to document the oral history of the shapers and makers of the art, to give other oral historians an outlet for their documents, and to make these oral histories available to the public. Since 1976, *Cadence* has published approximately 400 oral history projects. I would invite individuals interested in taking or reading oral history to contact me directly at *Cadence Magazine,* The Cadence Building, Redwood, N.Y. 13679 (315 287-2852).

If you enjoy the music of these individuals, their oral history will give you further insights into and enjoyment of the music. If you are not familiar with the individual's music, I'd strongly suggest immediate investigation. Both the music and oral history are the stuff of Jazz history and this is basically a Jazz history book.

Bob Rusch
June 1983

Most of the material in this book appeared in somewhat different form in *Cadence Magazine: The American Review of Jazz and Blues*. Cadence, The Cadence Building, Redwood, N.Y. 13679, is a recommended source for information and reading for anyone seriously interested in the art of improvisation.

Freddie Hubbard

Freddie Hubbard was born in Indianapolis, Indiana, March 7, 1938. He has become one of the major stylistic influences on trumpet. Mr. Hubbard rose to prominence in the '60s and for a while was a member of Art Blakey's Jazz Messengers. In the '60s he was also part of two of the seminal New Music recordings of the so called "Free Jazz" revolution of that period. In 1960 he recorded, as a member of the Ornette Coleman Double Quartet, a 36-minute collective improvisation released by Atlantic Records as *Free Jazz* (Atlantic). Five years later, as a member of another specially hand-picked group, he recorded with John Coltrane a 37-minute collective improvisation called by the latter *Ascension* (Impulse 95). In 1970, after a decade of recording many fine records under his own name for the Blue Note, Impulse and Atlantic labels, he began a series of recordings for CTI Records which, while not without artistic merit, began increasingly to rely on commercial concessions. By the mid-'70s, when this interview was conducted, Mr. Hubbard, much to the discontent of Jazz purists, was recording music which was aimed directly at the commercial mass market. In the 1980s Mr. Hubbard has with increasing regularity returned to recording uncompromising improvised music. Surprisingly, he has shown a renewed brilliance in his abilities, recording material which is equal to some of his very best work.

I interviewed Mr. Hubbard in Montreal, Quebec in December 1975. I had prearranged with him to conduct the interview at his hotel in the afternoon. Mr. Hubbard did not show up at the appointed time and in fact completely stood me up, leaving me to cool my heels from 4 p.m. till 9 p.m. when he was scheduled to play at In Concert, a now defunct Montreal night club. Fortunately, Brownie McGhee was also in Montreal, and although I was not prepared in the way of researching my subject, I managed to connect with Mr. McGhee and do an interview with him while waiting to intercept the elusive Mr. Hubbard at the night club.

I arrived at In Concert early hoping to grab some interview time before the first set. Unfortunately, Mr. Hubbard arrived late. On arrival he greeted me with a perfunctory apology for not meeting me at his hotel. And while he removed his camel hair coat, grabbed his trumpet, acknowledged hangers on, all seemingly in one hectic motion, he suggested that perhaps we could do the interview between sets. Such interviews often produce no more than self-serving surface PR. However, I felt at least I could zero in on specific areas in which I had questions. Time limitations eliminated any chance for general probing.

Mr. Hubbard played a loud, electronically amplified, set which accurately reflected the rather sad commercial state of his music of that period. At the end of the set he announced that he had just been selected first in the *Down Beat Readers' Poll.*[1] *In fact,* it was Miles Davis, a leader of the Rock-Jazz fusion movement, who had placed first. It was on that note that the 20-minute interview began. It was the first interview printed in the first issue of *Cadence Magazine* (January 1976).

R.D.R.: What's this *Down Beat Readers' Poll* thing? You didn't win it this year.

F.H.: I didn't?

R.D.R.: No.

[1]A poll sponsored by *Down Beat Magazine* at the end of each year in which readers are asked to send in the name of their favorite artist for various instruments.

F.H.: Who won it?

R.D.R.: Miles.

F.H.: '75?

R.D.R.: You came in second.

F.H.: They told me I won it.

R.D.R.: What do those polls mean in real terms? Do they affect anything?

F.H.: Well, it's people showing their appreciation for the music. It makes you feel good; it's like an award.

R.D.R.: In 1961 you joined Art Blakey. How does that affect an individual artist? Many individual leaders have emerged from the Messenger groups.

F.H.: The thing with Art Blakey, the name Jazz Messengers—he's supposed to give you the message, you're supposed to carry it on. When ı first join Art Blakey's group he tells you, "Look, I don't expect you to stay with me forever, I'm just supposed to train you and then get you ready for the business as well as the music—how to handle and form a group."

R.D.R.: How was it different from working with Max Roach?

F.H.: Max Roach was like a highly individual thing; it wasn't a group effort at all. Like when you play with him, it was like you were on your own, you had to be way up on technique and together before he even got you. You'd play fast all night, it was up to you to keep up with him, because he was gone with the fast tempo. I think after the group he had with Clifford Brown, Harold Land, George Morrow and those guys, that group thing wasn't in his mind. He didn't care anymore, it was just getting some guys together who he wanted to play with. It was a thrill for me to play with him, 'cause I knew he was such a highly respected drummer who could teach me so much. Like I said, it was more an individual effort than with Art Blakey where it was like a team, ensemble playing.

R.D.R.: Max's outwardly, at least, a more political person.

F.H.: Yeah, he was very heavy into the political thing. He was a Black Nationalist at the time. I would say he devoted more of his time into that than he did his music. Which taught me something, too, 'cause he had me so uptight. I was very uptight about the racist thing, you know. I went to Europe and I made a speech—called everybody a White pasty-face devil. So the guy said, "Why are you bringing that shit over here, we ain't got that many Black people over here. You take that back to America." That was a period when I was very bitter, but now after I've read a few books and hanging out with different people, it kind of got my mind off that racist thing. One of the books was *Black Cargo* by James Rogers. It was my awareness of dealing with people just as people. At that time I was a racist. I wouldn't even sit here and talk to you without cussing you out. I've changed, now I love everybody—even George Wallace (laughter). Don't write that down 'cause you'll have the brothers come lookin' for me. Yeah, put that down. It doesn't matter, I'll start a little controversy.

R.D.R.: What happened in '68 with Joe Henderson, Louis Hayes and The Jazz Communicators?

F.H.: We had a corporation going then. We had three leaders and split the money, equal billing. But what happened was that my name was about the biggest at the time, so whenever we would appear at concerts or clubs, the club owner kept coming to me. I kept telling them, "You would have to discuss anything you want to say with the three of us." I think the other guys kind of resented that, which was not what I wanted, 'cause we were really tight, the three of us. I think the egos got involved here. It was a very good band, too.

R.D.R.: Did you do any recording with that group?

F.H.: We didn't, man. We had a chance to get a contract with Contemporary Records and some nice money, but we just couldn't make it.

R.D.R.: In the 1960s you participated in two historic recording dates: Ornette Coleman's *Free Jazz* , and John Coltrane's *Ascen-*

sion. What were the circumstances behind and leading up to that?

F.H.: At that time I was hanging out in the Village (New York), and we used to have sessions at Ornette's pad—people like Archie Shepp, Marion Brown and Ed Blackwell—I was with that crowd. Plus I was practicing to go with Coltrane. Quite naturally you get together with ideas. But when he (Ornette) called me to do the session, I told him "Man, I can't really get into that bag, so I rather you get someone else." "No, man, we need you for the strength," 'cause Don Cherry didn't play that (strong). I didn't want to make it at first, but it was a challenge. We rehearsed twice and the music was really interesting, 'cause that was the first time I had played songs without chord changes. We got it together on sound, it was based on sound and feeling, certain rhythmic patterns we would hit at the same time. I would say that was the most challenging date I ever made in my life. You would have to create ideas that you never created before. In other words, I couldn't depend on any of my old clichés. I had to come up with something totally different. If after Eric Dolphy soloed, if I were to come in playing like I was with Art Blakey, I would sound kind of out of context. All of a sudden, I had to come up with some new shit and I had a headache for about two weeks trying to figure this stuff out. It came off pretty good, but I still felt I was kind of out of context on that date. It was totally spontaneous.

The *Ascension* date—there was no rehearsal for that. I asked Trane, "Why do you call me up for this kind of music?" He told me he was going to do somethin' totally different than what he had been doing like on *Giant Steps* [2] and things like that. I finally got to the point where I could play more kinds of changes at that kind of tempo. I asked him why don't you call Dewey Johnson, those cats, 'cause they're way out. He said "Freddie you can play anything, so just come on."

The first take we made, I laughed—I mean it was really weird, funny to me. Everybody in there was laughin', 'cause it sounded like a bunch of noise. After we got into it he had four scales he

[2]A previous recording utilizing a more familiar improvisational structure.

had written. What we would do is play the melody (opening) and that was the end of it. Actually, after we played one note of the scale, everybody hit that note and then you played whatever you felt like off of that particular scale. I had a hell of a time making up stuff, again, you know. Mostly what I did was scream, I think that's what he wanted me to do was scream on top.

Yeah, everybody was into free-form playing, but I felt kind of good 'cause I knew McCoy Tyner and Elvin (Jones)[3] were here and they were hip to my thing.

R.D.R.: Both recordings had had two takes issued....

F.H.: We had two takes. I played my ass off on the first take (*Ascension*).

R.D.R.: The Atlantic second issue (first take) is shorter than the original release (second take).

F.H.: I remember him (Ornette) stopping it 'cause the guys started trying to play like on a mode, and he (Ornette) didn't like that. He didn't want no modes or nothing. They wanted it to be completely different than anything that had been done before, and that's what he was concentrating on. I would say during that period, when he first came to New York, he revolutionized music. When he came in everybody was be-bopping—(Thelonious) Monk, Miles (Davis). He came in with this broken rhythm playing and everybody say, "What?" But he got the endorsement of people like John Lewis, Gunther Schuller, George Russell, and everybody said, "Wow!" Everybody was dying to sit in with Ornette in L.A., and he gave me a headache.

R.D.R.: During the *Ascension* date was there that feeling of explosion that comes across in the recording?

F.H.: Yeah, 'cause, see, Trane just lifted everybody up. He put us in a circle and he was standing where he could see all of us. Everybody was lookin' at him. The spirit, everybody just felt him and they started playing, he just lifted everybody up. It was

[3]Tyner (piano) and Jones (drums), were regular members of the John Coltrane group of the period.

like love, 'cause if you didn't love a cat you wouldn't be up there blowing your brains out, 'cause half the stuff just sound like everybody was playin' on top there for a minute. Like you said, when it exploded everybody was just up there, you know the feeling, and the power and all that was just up in the air. We looked at Trane, he was blowing his brains out, bend his knees, you could feel he was really sincere about it. So that in turn made you go ahead and try to do something. I mean he wasn't bullshittin', he was playin' licks, wasn't just screamin'. I think that's what a lot of tenor players miss—they don't get the true essence of what he was doing. They think he was screamin' but he was playing ideas. He was nuts about music. He was very hard to talk to on a general conversation basis 'cause all he wanted to talk about was the music. I think he got into other planets.

R.D.R.: What were the circumstances in 1970 with *Song of Songmy?* [4]

F.H.: I was at Atlantic Records at the time and my contract was out and I was trying to figure a way to get away from them 'cause they were trying to turn me into a Rock 'n' Roll cat then. I really didn't want to play that kind of music at that time. Quite naturally I rebelled, but I owed them a date. There was a guy producing at Atlantic Records, Ilhan Mimaroglu. He was into electronic music, and teaching at Columbia University, and he approached me with the idea: "Let's get involved with what's happening in the world politically and socially." He's a very heavy cat, but I didn't know at first if I wanted to deal with that electronic music 'cause some of it's not really music, just sounds. Every sound isn't music. I took the music home, I like challenges, and he had me playing a lot of intervalic playing. It was something different—it was more his idea—I just had to get the band together to pull it off. It didn't sell anything. They

[4] "A Fantasy for Electromagnetic Tape," released in 1971 by Atlantic (1576). It was released under Hubbard's name and featured him with his group playing the music and concept of Ilhan Mimaroglu. A concept recording, it dealt critically with the Vietnam War.

censored the record for two years, they said it was un-American. I really dug the record but it didn't get to the radio stations.

R.D.R.: Why did you leave Atlantic?

F.H.: Atlantic's just like most companies—if you sell, they keep you. In order to sell records today you find yourself fusing Jazz and Rock together. They kind of shied away from the harder playing groups. They wanted to make it commercially. CTI I think was the best recording period I had so far. Creed Taylor is a hell of a producer. I don't like him that much as a record company owner, I liked him as a producer. He always wanted you to do a tune (with the other CTI artists). So this was breaking up bands while we were out on a tour. Plus he had the same arrangers, the same musicians, on every session, so I got tired of it.

R.D.R.: Have you considered marketing your own music?

F.H.: I think if I get me a hit record I'm going to put out and try it, but it's going to take some capital.

R.D.R.: If all things were equal and you could record anything or play the way you wished, would you be playing the kind of material that you're presently doing on Columbia?

F.H.: No... simple as that, I wouldn't.

R.D.R.: How does the performer, specifically, see the record business?

F.H.: I know it's still a racial thing. I've seen other companies give Rock groups $100,000 up front to get all the funny equipment, uniforms and all, and then the group's a flop. I'm established, but I can't get any of that money. They don't think it's Madison Avenue. I've found out that also if I would hire one White cat in the band, I would be working in concerts—I know that. I don't really think it depends upon the color of the cat playing—I like Bill Evans, Stan Getz—but they put it on that level in most cases. What I think has got to happen is Black cats have to try and get their resources together and start producing

Jazz. I went to Barry Gordy,[5] now he's in a position to produce Jazz, but he said, "Man, it's not sellin'," but yet he's distributing Creed's records. It's going to take a hell of a change.

R.D.R.: On your last album you're listed as producer—how important is that?

F.H.: I learned something about the business end of it. I learned the cost, how to fill out the forms, cut cost, and how they made their money. Even after they give you $100,000 or $200,000 in advance you can be sure they're going to make double that before you get a penny. Being a producer sometimes conflicts with a personal relationship with a musician.

[5]The founding head of Motown Records, which for a while in the '70s distributed CTI Records.

Paul Quinichette

Paul Quinichette was born in Denver, Colorado, in 1916. His career has spanned playing with territory bands such as Nat Towles and Lloyd Hunter in the '30s, playing Rhythm 'n' Blues in the '40s, and recording with John Coltrane in the '50s. In the early '50s he joined the Count Basie band where his cool, laconic sax style got him nicknamed "Vice Pres" because the style was so similar to that of Lester Young,[1] who was known as "Pres." After leaving Basie, Mr. Quinichette worked with Benny Goodman and then dropped out of active playing, working in various nonmusical jobs. In the '70s he reappeared on the New York scene and still remains active into the '80s. I felt that Mr. Quinichette had too often been dismissed as a Lester Young copycat. I had enjoyed his playing for many years and was aware that the press had done little to document his story. I located Mr. Quinichette in New York City; I think this pleased me as much as it astonished him that anyone would travel hundreds of miles in the winter to interview him. Because I felt basic documentation was missing on the subject, I chose to dwell more on developing his oral history rather than directing specific limiting questions to him.

[1]Lester Young and Coleman Hawkins are each credited as the developer and fountainhead of the two great tenor sax styles; imprecisely summed up as the cool (Young) and hot (Hawkins) styles.

We conducted the interview in the uptown New York City apartment of his friend. It was a relaxed and warm meeting.

NOTE: Just after I wrote the above introduction, I learned that Paul Quinichette died in a New York City hospital on May 25, 1983.

P.Q.: I was born May 17, 1916. My mother got me a clarinet when I was about seven, a metal clarinet from Montgomery Wards (laughter), 35 bucks. She said "I'll buy this old metal one 'cause you might not want it." I played it all the time.

My mother used to send me to school with a tam on and knickers and a clarinet under my arm, looked like Buster Brown (laughter).

My father died in 1929, he was a doctor, a surgeon; my mother worked for an insurance company, she's retired. She worked up to the chairman of the board. She started out as the head of the stenographic department, and it blossomed out into a great big million dollar insurance company. It's a Negro insurance company called American Woodman. At first she was mad at me 'cause she wanted me to be like dad is, a doctor and that. She'd say, "Aw, you tootin' that darn old horn"—she didn't go for that at all and it took me a long time to convince her. I remember one time I got an old Buescher, silver alto. I had one before and she took it away from me; I don't know what she did with it. So there was a Jewish pawn shop in Denver. He had this silver Buescher hangin' up in there. I didn't have the money to get it so I said, "Listen, if I come in here and work, will you give me this horn?" He said, "Yeah." So he had me washing windows, polishing these rings and trays in the window. I was almost 16 then, but I got the horn. She (my mother) said, "Well, I'll be damned, if you can do this all right, I won't bother you no more." She used to kid me, "You goin' toot your old horn like Louis Armstrong?" I said, "Are you kiddin'?" (laughter). I wish I could.

R.D.R.: Were you taking lessons?

P.Q.: Yes, I was taking lessons on the clarinet and alto. On the clarinet I had a German teacher, I forget his name, he wrote all the stuff for us. He'd write everything for us we were weak at and if you didn't take this home and practice, when you'd come back, he'd crack your knuckles and fine my mother 35 cents (laughter).

R.D.R.: Classical?

P.Q.: Yeah, I had to know this for chord changes, basic harmonies. Then I had another fellow teach me alto, a White fellow from Oklahoma City. His name was Jim Story, and he could play that horn, get all over it. He didn't have the beat or swing, but he could play. I used to have an old victrola that you had to crank up and it had a thing on there to control the speed. So I'd play along with the records and I could change to any key I wanted to, slower speed was a different key. I was doin' all that—I had a lot of fun.

R.D.R.: When did you leave Denver?

P.Q.: I must have left... '38, along in there somewhere, '37 or '38. I had gigs there, there were a lot of places to play. There was one fellow who had a gambling house on the top and downstairs, he'd call it the hole, the band would come down there and play. I think we'd get something like $3 a night at those times. Then I left and went with Lloyd Hunter and his Territory Band. I must have been 18 or 19.

R.D.R.: How'd that come about?

P.Q.: I met a friend of mine named Preston Love; he'd came to Denver and he was working with Lloyd. He said, "Listen, I'll see if I can get you a job with Lloyd, can't do anything staying in Denver all the rest of your life, you'd be submerged." So that's what I did and my mom was screaming and wailing (laughter) about me going there. Anyway these guys traveled around Nebraska, Iowa, North Dakota, South Dakota, all that area, playing Jazz music. In those days a band would have these sleeper buses, you couldn't sit down you had to lay down. One band I was with there was one little old heat pipe going down the aisle. Your feet would burn up while you were freezin' on top (laughter).

R.D.R.: How were the Territory days?

P.Q.: Oh, they were just ordinary one-night stands, nothing spectacular about it; we had a lot of fun playing and the audiences liked us. For those days the bands were like a family, it wasn't like now where everybody out for themselves. It was like a family, each looking out for each other. I enjoyed it—you don't see it anymore.

R.D.R.: You also played with Ernie Fields' Territory Band, right?

P.Q.: Back then with Ernie Fields' Territory Band we went out there with Bojangles.[2] I hated that. It was Bojangles' show, he hired the band to back him up, he was the boss. He was like a dictator, and he had his Uncle Tom qualities, like Louis Jordan, I didn't like that at all. He'd sit up there and tell all these awful jokes. He'd get up there on the stage and say, "What's this?" and open his teeth and turn around and around. "I bet you don't know what this is?" People say, "No, no, what is it?" "That's a lighthouse." Those kind of things burned me up (laughter). He'd dance 75 blocks down the street backwards before he go into the theater—backwards! He had honorary police badges from all over the country—south, east, west, we didn't get close to him. I remember one time this guy beat him in pool. He always thought he was so great at playing pool. So this guy let him win and then he started beatin' Bojangles for one hundred, two hundred dollars a game. It was Minnesota Fats (laughter). He wanted to shoot him. That must have been in '39 and we were in Minneapolis.

R.D.R.: How long did you stay with the Territory Band?

P.Q.: I guess till around 1941. Then I joined Jay McShann's band. A lot of times we used to go to Kansas City and that's when I first heard the band. He had Charlie Parker, Gene Ramey, Al Hibbler and Gus Johnson playing for him. One of Jay McShann's tenor players left, 'cause his wife didn't want him on the road, so I got into the band. I stayed with him during the war. During

[2]The great dancer "Bojangles" Bill Robinson.

those times they took the buses away from the bands, and the Army personnel got on the trains first. Sometimes we rent some station wagons that had retreads on them that would last only 50 miles.

R.D.R.: What was your first impression on hearing Charlie Parker?[3]

P.Q.: At that time he was playing so well, I really dug him and I dug the old man who taught him also—Buster Smith; Charlie was a pupil of his; you hear him now (Buster Smith) and he sounds just like him. His teeth are gone now but that's where Charlie Parker got that from, the sound and the fingering. Charlie got better and better. Ruby Williams of the Savoy Sultans and Scoops Carey with Fatha Hines, when they heard him (Parker), he just fractured all of us (laughter), didn't know what way to go, we'd never heard anything like that. He was playing all the time. He'd be playing all night long and still be jamming at 10 or 11 the next morning. See, then Kansas City was really the hub of Jazz, Swing—4 Beat. It wasn't New York. New York was too cold and sophisticated.

R.D.R.: How was McShann to work for?

P.Q.: No trouble at all; he's like Basie, no trouble. A lot of people don't realize how much piano this guy can play, Jay McShann. I left him when we went to play San Francisco and then Los Angeles, and that's when I left him to join Johnny Otis who sounded so good to me.

R.D.R.: This was when Otis had the band.

P.Q.: Yes, and he had a little girl singin' with us. She wasn't but 14, called her Little Esther (Phillips) and we had to have a tutor go out with us on the road. It was a Basie-structure sound; he

[3]Charlie Parker, nicknamed "Bird" (1920-55), the great alto sax player whose brilliant playing and harmonic genius was largely responsible for ushering in and sustaining the revolutionary New Music of the '40s known as Bebop, or Bop. Parker ranks as one of the greatest innovators in the history of creative improvised music and there is little contemporary Western music which has not in some manner been touched by Parker's influence.

loved Basie. At that time Preston Love, who I worked with before with Lloyd Hunter, he was with Basie's band. Preston would write out some of the (Basie's) arrangements and give them to us. Sometimes the band would be off and Preston go get all of the arrangements out of the book and have them copied and give them to Johnny Otis. One time he gave one to Georgie Auld, a tune called "Taps Miller" and Basie heard it and said, "Hey, wait a minute, this guy got my own arrangement before I recorded it." Georgie had sold it note for note; Basie was so flabbergasted (laughter). I often wonder what happened to Georgie, I don't see him anymore. We had another horrible experience (with the Otis Band). We went out with the Ink Spots for about a year, with Slappy White and June Richmond. It was the Ink Spots' show and they hired us to back them up on it. They paid us all right, but I didn't care for it. We had a dressing room just for gambling, shot dice all day long. Slappy White would beat Bill Kenny (Ink Spot) all the time. Kenny called the police, tried to arrest Slappy, said that he was cheatin' (laughter). They made a lot of money though. Then we went back into California and we (Otis Band) couldn't get booked, no offers.

When I left Johnny's band, Benny Carter hired me. Then he went back to MGM, and I went to work with Big Sid Catlett at a place called "The Streets of Paris" with Marlow Morris on piano and John Simmons on bass. Then after that, that's when I got with Louis Jordan and came to New York. Another band which I hated all the time I was with him—Louis Jordan and his Tympany Five (laughter). I didn't like the type of thing he was doing, it wasn't Swing. I think Louis was a prelude to this Rock thing. I didn't like all those tunes— "Deacon Jones," "Caledonia," "Run Joe" and all that, but they were all hits. The money was great with him.

Louis' tenor saxman was sick, I think he had tuberculosis, and he wanted either me or Wardell Gray. Wardell was working somewhere and his wife didn't want to go, so I went with him. We went all over the place, all over the South, all over New York, everywhere, we even made a little old movie, a three reeler. I got sick of wearing those sequined, Christmas-tree uniforms, red pants, livid green coats, sequined ties and boots and we had to stand up there and dance and play those tunes. We fell out. I told him one time "Listen, you were doing much better when you were playin' first alto with Chick Webb than doin' this." He didn't like that at all, so that was a parting of the ways right there.

I left his band I think it was '48 and I was living with some of the guys in Dizzy Gillespie's band, sharing an apartment. They had gone to the Royal Roost[4] so I joined Hot Lips Page and worked off and on with him and Red Allen. Henry Red Allen was doing Dixieland Blues which was all right, but I didn't care for that too much 'cause I'm really a Kansas City type, 4-Beat swinger. After that I got with Basie.

R.D.R.: How'd you land with Basie?

P.Q.: At that time, must have been 1950, Wardell Gray was in the band and before me they had Don Byas and Lucky Thompson. Basie didn't care for Lucky. One day Wardell came by and said, "Listen man, come on and join the band, 'cause Basie wants you to play that seat." So I went on with them. At that time the band was not doing well and they cut down to a small group.

R.D.R.: You were there when the Basie band broke up. How did that come about and what was that like?

P.Q.: When they broke up we were working out in Las Vegas, a place called the Flamingo, I think it was in '51. There were a couple of junkies in the band, three or four in the brass section. Basie called them the Flying Black Aces 'cause when they were supposed to come in they'd be in a nod, asleep, so when we got through at the Flamingo, he fired the whole band. The whole band! (laughter) When we got the pay he had a note in the pay envelope—"This is it" (laughter). So he sent everybody back to New York. The whole bit. It hit us like between the eyes, we had no indication he was going to do that. He called me and Freddie

[4]The Royal Roost along with Birdland were two of the most important *downtown* Jazz clubs in the '50s.

Green, to call when we got into New York and tell him where we were. So he sent me a plane ticket to Chicago, and when I got there I said, "Where's the band?" There was only me and Marshall (Royal) and Clark Terry (laughter). "What happened to the band, man?" I was so surprised. Then while we were with this small group Dinah Washington was working around the corner from us. She came over and said, "Basie, is it all right if I use some of the cats in the band?" That's when I made those records with Dinah Washington for Mercury.

R.D.R.: Why did you leave the Basie band?

P.Q.: Well, the idea was when I started making records of my own, and some of them sold fairly well. So Basie says, "Why don't you leave the band and let me personally manage you. I'll have it all fixed; if it don't work, it just don't work." That was the set-up, then here comes James C. Petrillo,[5] sent me a telegram and Basie a telegram says, "I fine you both $20,000 'cause no band leader can make a monopoly out of his ex-sidemen." He stopped us cold, Petrilllo. Then Basie said all right I'll put it in Katherine's name, his wife. Petrillo sent us the same thing over and over again. "You can't put it in a wife's name." So I was out of the band a long time and I can't just go back there and take this job away from who had followed me, so I just kept my own band. Some of the dates I recorded, he (Basie) was playin' with me.

R.D.R.: Since then you more or less freelanced?

P.Q.: Yeah.

R.D.R.: You've worked with Benny Goodman who's reputed to have quite a temper; how did that go?

P.Q.: Well, he's mellowed now. I worked with him 10 or 15 years ago down in Ralph Walkins' Basin Street. Now he's completely different, he's tellin' jokes all the time, he's happy now, but then we used to call him "The Ray." He doesn't like the guys in the band to get much above him.

[5]Head of the Musicians Union.

R.D.R.: You didn't work with Charlie Christian did you?

P.Q.: No, but I knew him. The first time I met Charlie Christian he was working with a girl in Oklahoma named Anna May Windburn, who later on had the "International Sweethearts of Rhythm." I saw him later and he remembered me. Then he got tuberculosis and Benny (Goodman) put him in the hospital, but he'd sneak out and go jamming. He'd still be alive, I imagine, if he had of done what they told him to, but he'd sign himself out and play all night someplace. He just enjoyed playin' and that's it. I don't think he realized how other people viewed him. Guys like him and Jimmy Blanton, Fred Beckett—I don't think they were really aware of how much influence they had.

R.D.R.: Who is Fred Beckett?

P.Q.: He was a fantastic trombone player. He worked with Lionel Hampton; he had tuberculosis too, fantastic on the trombone. Nobody probably knows who he is, it's been so long since he's dead, he was getting over that horn so fast, way before J.J. (Johnson). He was faster than Vic Dickenson, in those days—he was pretty fast. This must have been in the '40s. (Note: Rust lists one date with Beckett in 1941 with Hampton.)

R.D.R.: You never did work with Hampton.

P.Q.: No, I never did want to work with Lionel Hampton. He had his horrible wife, Gladys, she was a monster (laughter). She hired everybody, not him. Tyree Glenn used to tell me about Lionel. He was a kick drummer, slide down stairs and stuff. Gladys says, "Why don't you be like Tyree." 'Cause she was polished and sophisticated. That's why he started to play the vibes. She made him study something else. See, Lionel was a drummer, he can still play the hell out of them right now.

R.D.R.: Let's talk about Lester Young.

P.Q.: Lester was in Denver, Colorado; he was working for a band named Art Bronson. Also at that time during those days Andy Kirk was a mailman; even Paul Whiteman lived out there for a long time. Art Bronson was in this night club. It was one of these kinds of bands that works there ten or twelve years.

Lester was ten years older than me and he was in Denver working with Art Bronson. He left there; he went to Fletcher Henderson's band and Fletcher fired him 'cause he didn't sound like Coleman Hawkins, and he came back to Denver crying at me, then later he got with Basie.

I went out to hear Art Bronson, I must have got home about four in the morning and I was about 16 and got hell from my mom; she raised hell with me (laughter).

I just went up to Lester and said I like the way he sounds. He was always nice. I had this crystal set and we'd listen to this guy playing this tenor...what a sound he'd get. It was actually Frankie Trumbauer playing a "C" melody, we found out later.

R.D.R.: You knew Pres before, during, and after his Basie days, what happened?

P.Q.: I think that World War II took a lot out of him.

R.D.R.: Did he ever talk about it?

P.Q.: Yeah, see he didn't play that soldier, he rebelled against it. They cut his hair off like a bowl haircut and put him in the stockade. I don't know, he must have told one of his officers to go to hell or something. He said, "They told me I was insubordinate and they put me in the stockade." When he came out of it he was shook. Lester never used stuff or anything like that, just gin. After he came out of the war he was still playing wonderfully. Then he got his teeth extracted and he never got that other sound with false teeth, but it was still a pretty sound.

R.D.R.: Was he drinking a lot with the Basie band?

P.Q.: No, not too much, maybe a little bourbon when they took a break. After the war he lost his appetite, he wouldn't eat anything. I tried to get him to eat, nobody could get him to eat and he started drinking a lot of gin. Sometimes he'd get a Chinese dinner and just sit there and look at it. He told me one time that when he was in the stockade one time that Lee (brother) took his clothes and sold his horn; that was a dirty trick.

I'd go by his place four, five or six in the morning and I didn't know he was that sick. I was working up to Basie's lounge and he was down there in a hotel, across from Birdland, died right there in his bed. I don't know what happened, maybe it was his liver.

R.D.R.: Do you think he was relieved?

P.Q.: I don't think so; if there's a hereafter he's probably surprised as hell (laughter). A lot of people say he was trying to kill himself; I never went for all that. Everyone got some old horrible jaded outlook—"Oh, he's been trying to kill himself for years." I don't think he was trying to kill himself. They say the same thing about Billie Holiday. I worked for her; it just wasn't so.

Lester was no more trying to kill himself than the man in the moon. He was drinkin' and having fun, he liked to play, he just lost his appetite. Everytime I saw him he seemed to be enjoying himself. I'd see him, talk to him on the phone. I think he had a lot of wife trouble. The last thing he would look for was sympathy; he didn't need it.

He had a sister, her name was Irma, and at one time I had a crush on her. She was living out in Los Angeles and she was a heck of an alto saxophone player. You'd be surprised how she could play it. She got married and gave it up, she didn't want to do it no more.

Lee, his brother, has always been more sophisticated. He always worked with MGM or studio bands like that. He's still workin', he's always got something goin', he more of a business-man than Lester or Irma was.

R.D.R.: How much of his life was tied up with Billie Holiday, what was the relationship as you saw it?

P.Q.: Well, she was crazy about him—it was more like a brother-sister, maybe a lover there, but she loved him. They were very close.

R.D.R.: What was your picture of Billie Holiday as contrasted with the public picture?

P.Q.: The book written by Dufty (*Lady Sings the Blues*), that was terrible. Now he didn't write that correctly, he wrote just what he thought, an offhand picture, a different person; some of the critics will get things so messed up it's completely out of perspective. It's something else, it's another thing goin' on.

R.D.R.: What was Billie Holiday to you?

P.Q.: Well, I think she was very nice, she was very good to me. Actually she paid me more money than Basie, to tell the truth. It was very enjoyable working for her. I remember one time where she stopped drugs completely. We were playing over in Philadelphia and she had the narcotic agents come and sit in her dressing room so they couldn't tell some more lies on her about it. They came in and sat with her. During that time Chet Baker was on the bill with her and he saw the narcotic thing goin' on and he got scared and ran off, took all the money and left his band stranded there. That was at Pepe's Bar in Philadelphia. So he was doing pretty good. After I left there I don't know what happened or who got to her. People always trying to have the prestige of being with Billie Holiday.

R.D.R.: Was she bitter?

P.Q.: No, she was happy. I never saw her bitter about anything. She was tough to anybody she didn't know. Sometimes nuts would come back to her, "Give me a little hoot," she'd be really disturbed, tell them to get lost. But people she knew, like guys in the band, she was just a doll. Naturally anybody singing that long, your voice wouldn't be the same it was when you're 19, but it didn't detract that much. This movie company wanted to do her life story and they wanted Dorothy Dandridge to play it. Well, Dorothy Dandridge looked at that script, she says, "This is ridiculous, this is not Billie Holiday." She turned it down. So years later they got this thing here from the Supremes (Diana Ross) to do it—it's probably the same script Dorothy Dandridge wouldn't do, she said, "This is not right! You're making Lady look like nothin', I won't do it." She actually turned it down. Diana Ross did the best she could but still... but that was a pure business caper... when a person's dead. It won't be long they'll do Lester and then Coleman Hawkins, Paul Gonsalves. These guys will take the money and put it in their pocket.

R.D.R.: How long did you work with her?

P.Q.: I went out on the road with her for about a year. I was backing her up, introducing her, bringing her up on the stand. I usually played before, with the group. She'd stand over in the wings until she got ready to come on, then she'd wave her finger, we'd take the number out and introduce her to the people.

R.D.R.: Did your sound develop from Lester Young or develop parallel to it?

P.Q.: I think it was parallel to it, I think it came from both Trambauer and Pres. I had known Lester for so long, way before his Basie days. I knew his family, he knew my family, we always liked each other, I was always there with him—so it came out that way. It just came natural 'cause I was there.

R.D.R.: Are you tired of the comparisons with Pres?

P.Q.: No, I'm not tired of it, it's going to be here, that's it. Actually this guy down there at Birdland, Oscar Goodstein, nicknamed me Vice Pres. I say to people, listen, this is Paul playing this horn right here, not Lester—it's me. I'm playing these notes, these concepts. See, I was closer to Pres from the beginning. Zoot Sims and Stan Getz, they actually emulated him. Actually Zoot's name is Jack Sims, that Zoot thing is when he came to New York from St. Louis with a zoot and all those big chains and all that.

R.D.R.: Do you listen to the new sax player?

P.Q.: I like Sonny (Rollins), Coltrane, they're a different breed.

R.D.R.: What became of Paul Quinichette during the '60s?

P.Q.: Well, I was having trouble being booked so I went to school at RCA. I was an electronic technician. At one time I went down to work on Wall St., during the summer. Dickie Wells said come on down, and Julian Dash was there. They (stock brokers) would hire you for summer replacements as a courier runner. I did that for about a month, then after that I started with the electronics. I got fed up with that, fixing color TV sets and gigging on the weekend.

I worked around Wall St. for a while, Dickie Wells said, "Listen, there're a lot of musicians doin' this. You take stocks over to another broker." There was nothing to it. I worked for Goodbody and Company and (Julian) Dash worked for Merrill Lynch. That must have been in the early '60s. Dickie Wells is still there right now and Julian Dash was there for years before he died. You'd be surprised how many guys are down there.

R.D.R.: There was no big band work?

P.Q.: All of a sudden the American people, they stopped dancing. All those ballrooms all across the country and theaters they all shut down, now some of them are supermarkets, some of them are churches. There's no place to put a big band. Now the thing is concerts and Europe. Americans take it for granted, Europeans are much more receptive. Race has a lot to do with it too. Listen, here for instance, if it's a choice of someone to hire, they'll hire Zoot Sims over me. He's a good player, but it's a thing you know. You'll get the second references, that's the way it goes. Sometimes we'll invent something they'll have to copy fast, figure it out and say they did it. On the other side, I think Benny (Goodman) and Woody (Herman), Artie Shaw and Charlie Bennett didn't care who you were as long as you could play. Charlie was something else, he'd interview everybody who wanted a job. He'd ask, "Do you drink?" and the guy would try to impress him, "No, I don't drink"—he wouldn't hire him (laughter), got to have something, even a little cocktail.

As of now I'm working as a single—now they hire you as an individual. They don't say such and such bands anymore, they call you on the phone, say would you like to play this date. Sometimes you go play and you don't know who you're playin' with. It's individual personalities.

Milt Jackson

Milt Jackson is one of the many fine musicians who come out of Detroit. Born in 1923, he joined Dizzy Gillespie in the mid '40s. He was the first to adapt the vibraharp to the Bop idiom and remains the premier, and most influential, vibes man on the scene today.

Milt Jackson has recorded numerous records and worked in many contexts since the '40s, but he is best known as a founding member of the Modern Jazz Quartet, which was formed in the early '50s and remained, until its breakup in 1974, one of the most resilient and long-lasting groups in Jazz. With the exception of Connie Kay's replacing the original drummer (Kenny Clarke) in 1955, the group remained unchanged over the years (Jackson, vibes; Kay, drums; John Lewis, piano; Percy Heath, bass). In the early '80s the group once again began performing with regularity in public.

This interview was conducted in March 1977, after the initial breakup of the MJQ and at a time when rumors of its reuniting were being circulated in the industry. At the time of the interview Mr. Jackson was appearing at a New York City night club. The interview was conducted comfortably between sets while Mr. Jackson consumed with ardor a sizeable meal which among other things consisted of mussels and Italian bread.

R.D.R.: Let's get the obvious question out of the way. You may or may not have heard the rumor on the street that the MJQ is regrouping.

M.J.: Yeah, I've heard it, and let me immediately clarify it 'cause it's become a normal thing by now. It's not a resurgence by the quartet at all, it's a commitment I made to fulfill, at an appropriate time, which will be soon, I'm merely fulfilling the commitment. But as for a regrouping or getting back together . . . no. This is the last one, I am merely fulfilling a commitment.

R.D.R.: Many people would think that a steady gig would have its advantages. What are the advantages of being on your own.

M.J.: Two main factors: peace of mind—which I have much more of now, which I will never give up again—and far more money to top it off.

R.D.R.: More money?

M.J.: I make more money now than I did then.

R.D.R.: What do you mean by peace of mind?

M.J.: I'm talking about peace of mind musically. If you can understand that.

R.D.R.: I can understand that, but on the other hand I've always enjoyed Milt Jackson whether it was with Horace Silver, Sonny Rollins, alone and with the Modern Jazz Quartet.

M.J.: Let me see if I can enhance the statement a bit by saying I feel more relaxed, my thoughts are clearer. I don't have any kind of middle person of any sort. Peace of mind breaks down into what an individual thinks is peace of mind. I think I know what mine is, I've found it and like I said, I will never give it up again.

R.D.R.: The embryo of what later became the MJQ came out of Dizzy Gillespie's band with what could be looked upon now as the first Milt Jackson Quartet.

M.J.: It actually was my group. The reason for the incorporation was when John (Lewis) decided to go to Manhattan and finish and get his masters, he didn't want to bill no one else by individual name if it wasn't going to be himself, which I could not blame him for. So we collaborated on a group name and this is how it happened. You know there are a couple of other things I'd like to discuss other than my background. That's the fact that it's never been pointed out that Jazz music has never had the 90 minutes on Friday night (TV) that the Rock people get on NBC. So for 37 years I've been beating my head against the wall trying to remain pure, let's say, creative, and it's like to no avail. It's understandable that a lot of the innovators are no longer living, so it's only natural that a trend would take place and it would be a different trend. Nobody will perfect Charlie Parker's style better than he did—things like this. Okay, that's fine, but my question is why? They had the Grammy the other night. As great as Sarah (Vaughan) is, she never won nothing. How come?

R.D.R.: But don't you know part of the answer?

M.J.: I know all the answers, but I want some of the laymen to know. Because the kids don't know why they go to the record shop and buy Elton John records. That's 'cause they hear it all the time. They would respond to Lester Young and Coleman Hawkins and all the rest, but they have never been exposed to it.

R.D.R.: But it's more than just that, it's a racial thing also.

M.J.: Yeah. That too, you see, when you introduce Doc Severinsen and Al Hirt as two of the greatest Jazz trumpeters in the world—82 thousand people standing there and 54 million more looking in—you can't win. So what does that make Dizzy? 'Cause he's one of the few still living. 'Cause for the years that I stayed with the quartet, that was my idea of making big money, 'cause Bach music wasn't my thing. Luckily I did have a classical background. Now we go back to peace of mind. In other words, man, I can play what I feel like playing. Any kind of piece I want to play, like I want to play it, my kind of style with no kind of hang-up whether I miss a note or not. John had a well, methodical, planned program. Nothing wrong with it, but it just wasn't mine. I only could put a certain part of my own personality into it. This way I can use all of my own personality, 'cause it's my own thing.

R.D.R.: Why did you stay for 23 years then?

M.J.: 'Cause I thought we were going to get rich and make money. That's the only reason I put on that tuxedo every night.

R.D.R.: You know, as I was watching you play I wondered if Milt Jackson has a closet full of tuxedos at home—just sittin'—that he's never going to wear.

M.J.: Listen, since you brought it out, let me ask you a very pointed question—isn't that the most uncomfortable and stiffest feeling you've ever had in your life? Well, can you imagine me doing it every night. Listen, after I got out of that I may never wear a tuxedo again in my whole life. (Laughter).

R.D.R.: But there must have been some satisfaction with the MJQ.

M.J.: Hey, there's a lot of musical satisfaction, sure, most definitely. My theory man, is you use anything. You can always use it one of two ways, sometimes three. That is to an advantage or to a disadvantage. Now when you learn to live with something, I feel it's by outweighing the disadvantages with the advantages. I'd never deny there were many advantages in the group that could never be replaced, like the reputation for being gentlemanly. These kinds of things, and it carried a lot of weight. But it came down into a more personal level as for what's best for my family and for me and my future.

R.D.R.: Your earlier work seems to have a more metallic sound. Did you make a major change or adjustment in your instrument?

M.J.: Right, and it was a very horrible instrument. It was a long time before I could even afford a decent instrument to play on. It was a set of Leedys, made by the Leedy drum company. But I had a Jenco first. Then in '50 while I was still with Woody Herman I got the set I still have now. It's a pre-war Imperial made in 1937.

R.D.R.: But it's not a stock instrument.

M.J.: Not anymore, they don't make it anymore. What made that instrument so good is the fact it was made before the war and the material is so much better than post-war material. It had the electric speed control, and it took me a long time to figure out the correct sound and how to get it how I wanted it. Now the sound also comes from the fact when I was singing back in '39 and '40. The vibrato with the instrument is the type sound I use for my voice. In playing a ballad for example, the sound on the instruments is the same way I would always visualize myself as a vocalist.

R.D.R.: What were some of the first musical sounds for you?

M.J.: Well, if you wanted to go way back. It goes back to when I was seven, when I started listening to tunes on the radio and stuff, playing them on my piano and on my guitar, which was actually my first instrument, by the way. It was either Gospel music or Country and Western.

R.D.R.: Sanctified music?

M.J.: Yeah, very much so.

R.D.R.: What was the Detroit environment in the early '40s when you got started?

M.J.: It was a beautiful environment then. I wish they could have kept that environment and enhanced it. The environment of the '40s in Detroit was very similar to the environment of 52nd Street when I first came to New York. That was also a very memorable occurrence for me, something completely unforgettable and something I never figured would be destroyed like it did. In the radius of one block that was between Fifth Avenue and Sixth Avenue you could catch any number of artists. You could go at nine and at four when the nightclubs closed and you still couldn't catch it all. That was it for me. In Detroit we had Al McKibbon, Howard McGhee, Teddy Edwards, who actually moved to the West Coast, the Jones brothers.

R.D.R.: You had a group called the Four Sharps...

M.J.: Yeah, that's a group we organized when I got out of the service in '44.

R.D.R.: A vocal group?

M.J.: No, it wasn't, although we did commercial vocals within the group, like I sang and the bass player sang. I was playing vibes then and bass, piano and guitar. In fact the bass player and myself are the only ones left, the other two passed away.

R.D.R.: You made a strictly vocal album in Europe?

M.J.: Yeah, in '64 in Italy. A complete vocal album, except for one track I played a piano solo. I have the rights to it for release in the States and Canada, but never got around to it. The reason I didn't follow it up is because I didn't want to be a victim of the conflict the same we got going with Nat Cole with his. Because of him becoming commercial as a singer for Capitol Records, people didn't know how "bad" he was as a piano player. That was a philosophy of my father's, "Don't be no jack of all trades, be good at one thing." And when I chose to play I forgot about the singing, and this is really why I didn't follow it up because I didn't want people to think that I wanted to capitalize in terms of a gimmick or something like that. Music has always been too serious for that kind of thing.

R.D.R.: You were with CTI Records for a short period of time. Was there an effort there to put you into a more commercial setting?

M.J.: All companies, and I do mean *all*, invariably get caught up in that situation where they want you to try and exist commercially, because most of them, regardless of how dedicated they may feel, they're interested in making money. This is most of the hassle I had with all the companies up till the present company I'm with now (Pablo).

R.D.R.: But were you also trying to make an effort in that direction?

M.J.: I tried, not so much for my benefit as for others'. Actually what I did it for was to try and convince them it is not for every musician or every artist to make the transition, and every artist cannot successfully make the transition. I was satisfied that we did mostly what we could do under the circumstances, and from a commercial point of view, it got us as far as winning an award from *Stereo Magazine* as one of the best albums of 1975, for what that's worth.

R.D.R.: Do you still involve yourself with the piano much?

M.J.: Not too much, only now when I want to write. I'm getting more heavily involved in writing 'cause I formed a new company, Reecie Music; I've been involved in trying to get a lot of material to try and build the company up.

R.D.R.: Are there any particular recordings you've made which you are most satisfied with.

M.J.: Yeah, the first string album (Atlantic) I did with Quincy I thought was really nice, and this last one with Jimmy Jones' arrangements, "Feelings." In fact, the reason I did the "Feelings" was because of the album I did with Quincy years ago. Also the album called "Big Bags" on Riverside where Tadd Dameron did the arrangements on one side and Ernie Wilkins the other.

R.D.R.: Any you were particularly dissatisfied with?

M.J.: I knew you'd get around to that. Now, do you remember the album, which we won a Grammy with, "That's The Way It Is: Live at Shelly's"? Okay, the same producer, I tried to get him to do a follow up album like that, live, 'cause that was the best chance. He insisted on me going into the studio and doing a Rock date, big band. I said, "Okay, man, but I don't think it's going to work." They got the arrangers, got the best cats to play that kind of stuff. Man, that was the worst date musically and financially I ever had in my life. "Memphis Jackson" was the name.

R.D.R.: How did the association with Apple Records ever come about?

M.J.: The Beatles, they loved the Quartet, and when they formed that company they asked us if we would do a couple of albums for them. They let us do whatever we wanted, they never interfered.

R.D.R.: Do you enjoy working for Pablo?

M.J.: So far it's been one of the most enjoyable because he has more respect than most producers have for the artists and the kind of music the artists want to play, which is very important. Most companies are caught up in that commercial turmoil. I just refuse to destroy the artistic quality of my music for the sake of making money. My thing is this: in order to have perseverance for my self, I believe you have to love this music... to see Sonny and Cher, for example—I don't think it takes great talent to do what they're doing, and yet they're making lots of money for it. I can't begrudge you the right to make a living as a human being, 'cause that's only natural, but, hey, give me a chance to. And we've never had it.

R.D.R.: And do you think you ever will on that level?

M.J.: I don't know, not while I'm here. I had hoped before I left some parts of it would happen. But unless we get 90 minutes of Jazz music on NBC, coast to coast, it's not going to happen; or play our music on American Bandstand and let the kids dance to that.

R.D.R.: You must have some satisfaction in knowing that the artistry of Milt Jackson will outlast a 100,000 Sonny and Chers.

M.J.: Right, that's the compensation, to know that my music will last far longer than that.

Cecil Taylor

Cecil Taylor was born in New York City in 1933. His music education includes time at the New York College of Music and the New England Conservatory as well as playing in New York with some of the post-Swing mainstream bands. Since the 1950s he has always led his own groups or appeared as a solo pianist and has remained active in the avant-garde of New Music since the mid 1950s. Though recognized as a unique innovator in the field of creative improvised music, it is only since the mid '70s that he has begun to receive any of the substantial rewards and recorded documentations that, even considering the general neglect given Jazz artists, is afforded to most musicians of his stature.

Through the years, a good deal of the press has been insensitive to Mr. Taylor's artistic statements even to the point of suggesting his music is anti-Jazz. He has developed a reputation with the media as being difficult to deal with. I have found in speaking with hundreds of creative improvising artists that the media has also developed a reputation as being difficult to deal with.

I arranged with Mr. Taylor to interview him in Montreal on February 19, 1978. Earlier in the day I had interviewed Jimmy Lyons, Mr. Taylor's long-time alto saxophonist. After that interview, I drove Mr. Lyons over to a reception given for Mr. Taylor and his group. Based on the reputation that preceded him, I had certain apprehensions about interviewing Mr. Taylor. As the reception progressed, it became later and later and Mr. Taylor seemed bored by the proceedings but made no overt suggestion that we leave to conduct an interview (Mr. Taylor has often refused to give interviews). Finally throwing caution aside, I good-naturedly began bullying Mr. Taylor and suggested that perhaps it was time to get on with what was no doubt the thing he most looked forward to, our interview. Punctuating my remarks by bumping my ample stomach into his shoulders (Mr. Taylor is rather small with the build and movement of a dancer), he responded with unenthusiastic resignation and we drove to his hotel where he had room service send up an egg salad sandwich and soda. By the time the interview ended, my trepidations had gone. I was left with the impression of a serious artist completely open for discussion.

R.D.R.: If you were the editor of a magazine, or you could control the media, how would you do it?

C.T.: (Laughter) I would present only major artists... major poets. I would present artists I felt were major.

R.D.R.: How would you handle criticism?

C.T.: The thing that would be working for me is the fact that for the last 20 years I've made it my business to find out who the artists were... and it didn't necessarily have to be in my field. Also helping me in the discretion that would be utilized would be the fact that being, attempting to be, a poet myself, it's my work.

R.D.R.: How important is the aspects of your poetry to you as a creative outlet relative to the music?

C.T.: It is, I think, music in print.

R.D.R.: Do you have a standard agreement with record companies about putting your poetry on the liner notes?

C.T.: It depends on the record company.

R.D.R.: Would you care to discuss...

C.T.: (Laughter).

R.D.R.: I've heard that your best-selling album to date has only sold 10,000 copies. I find that hard to believe. A fact?

C.T.: Uh huh, it was Montreux *The Silent Tongues*. But they're notoriously poor with their count, and they are even more notoriously slow in paying up.

R.D.R.: Do you think it's an unreasonable figure?

C.T.: Well I think they lie...either deliberately or for other reasons; they, of course, what they don't want to evaluate properly are sales in other places, in other countries.

R.D.R.: Is Unit Core[1] an active record company anymore?

C.T.: No.

R.D.R.: Do you own the masters to that material?

C.T.: Uh huh.

R.D.R.: There were only two records released. "Indents" was reissued on Arista. Are there any plans for "Spring of Two Blue Jays" to be reissued?

C.T.: I don't know what any record company has plans for. Will I sell it? I haven't thought about it.

R.D.R.: It's been said the Carnegie Hall concert you did with Mary Lou Williams[2] is going to be issued on Pablo.

[1] Unit Core was the name of a record label, no longer active, set up by Cecil Taylor to release his music.

[2] Mary Lou Williams (1910-1981): a leading Jazz pianist who came into Jazz prominence while working with the Andy Kirk Orchestra from the late '20s through the early '40s. Early on she embraced and reflected to some extent the developing modern Jazz (Bop) of the '40s. On April 17, 1977, Ms. Williams and Mr. Taylor appeared together in concert at Carnegie Hall. Music from that concert was eventually released on a two-record set on Norman Granz' Pablo (2620-108) with the ironic title "Embraced."

C.T.: Yes.

R.D.R.: That concert got less than enthusiastic reviews. How successful do you think it was?

C.T.: (After a long pause—laughter)... Completely successful.

R.D.R.: Were there many meetings between you and Ms. Williams before the concert?

C.T.: Yes.

R.D.R.: Did it come off the way you planned it?

C.T.: ... (Laughter)... Yeah, I knew what I was going to do.

R.D.R.: Are you aware of the general remarks given to the concert in the press?

C.T.: Yeah, sure, uh huh.

R.D.R.: Do you think they were fair?

C.T.: Well, I don't think fairness has anything to do with it. I think what you're dealing with predominantly... people who have concepts about music, who for the most part are not musicians and who are not really even good journalists... so ... they were bound to be disturbed... so was Miss Williams.

R.D.R.: She was disturbed?

C.T.: Yeah, she was disturbed by the concert, yeah.

R.D.R.: By the music end of it?

C.T.: My... yes, what I did.

R.D.R.: Was she surprised by it?

C.T.: Well, yes, she was... but then again we traded surprises that evening.

R.D.R.: She was not satisfied?

C.T.: I think she was, to put it modestly, I think she was outraged by it.

R.D.R.: What outraged her?

C.T.: My playing.

R.D.R.: In general? Stylistically?

C.T.: My playing that evening outraged her I think.

R.D.R.: Was it different from what one would expect from a Cecil Taylor concert?

C.T.: ...Nnnnn...ah, upon the surface I would suppose not ...but you see the real issue is that you can respect...and perhaps even love musicians, as I do, [of] a lot of different eras ...but finally what has to really be agreed upon is what music is and what the specifics of the tradition and how you want to apply it to a given situation...Ms. Williams had a particular idea in mind what she wanted to do and it seemed to me that ... it was really never understood on her part how I viewed ... music. It's very simple, most of the people thought, most of the critics thought that...there would be an attempt to reduplicate styles of eras gone past. I consider that possibly one way to do things. The other thing that came to me to feel about it was that the legacy of those preceding generations still lives, not only in the musical present of those people who are still alive from those generations, but the major principles of musical organizations that those people have given us are the property of all succeeding musical generations.

R.D.R.: A continuum?

C.T.: Yeah! And also it seems to me one has to be very careful about making the separation between style...and...musical creativity. See, because the total factors of historical environment that determine what style is...you know it's not about resurrecting a particular situation, artifacts from museums.

So, as I pointed out to Miss Williams in the evening before the concert when we rather heatedly discussed this matter...ah... I didn't see any Jelly Roll Morton...you know, the way she laid out the program, you know, I didn't see any James Reese

Europe. But when it came down to the issue of what music, it seemed to me that my responsibility was in any context to create music that I thought was valid, exists today paying homage to the preceding eras—but on my own terms.

The interesting thing, one of the reasons I finally decided to go along with that record—the publication of it, which I understand will be out in April. I have certain things that I decided after hearing the tape that Mary and her priest mastered which was completely unacceptable to me, I thought the original master was a very poor representation of what happened just in terms of the balance. And the Granz people were receptive to how I felt. If the record was going to be published, it should . . . certain things should be altered, and they agreed to it. The result was I remastered the concert and I also finally wrote some notes which I suppose will appear alongside Mary's. . . . I'm going to let it rest on the basis of what I wrote.

R.D.R.: She could have vetoed the release.

C.T.: No, she could not have. It was her idea to go to Granz in the first place. I said, right, always deferring to the lady. I said I didn't think it was a good idea. There were several people I was dealing with at the time that said I should do it. But the thing that finally persuaded me was when I heard the tape on a very good machine on which I could really hear what I was playing, because the way Mary had it done originally I was playing triple pianissimo throughout and ah . . . ah . . . ah . . . I say the concert was a success because I did exactly what I wanted to do. Including walking off the stage and letting Ms. Williams have three encores by . . . the group that she called in that I first played with six o'clock the evening of the concert.

R.D.R.: You didn't know there would be backing?

C.T.: Well, originally it was supposed to be a two piano . . . and the week before the concert I had some kind of flu, so in the middle of the week I was informed that Mary was bringing in a bass player and drummer. I didn't get a chance to play with them till six o'clock the evening of the concert, which I knew there was going to be a problem for them.

The obvious question, since Andrew Cyrille[3] worked, I believe, with Mary Lou Williams (before), it's curious that he was not asked to be the drummer.

R.D.R.: The press has generally characterized you as the heavy in this presentation at Carnegie.

C.T.: But that's not an unusual place for me to be... but of course I am heavy, but I'm not negatively heavy. But then I don't think particularly highly of the press.

R.D.R.: Do you like giving interviews?

C.T.: I try not to for the most part for a variety of reasons.

R.D.R.: On the "Spring of Two Blue Jays" you dedicated the poem and record to Ben Webster. Why?

C.T.: Well, fortunately I heard Ben Webster with the Ellington band in '66, which was the last time I heard him, alive, in London. And also fortunately I was given at a very early age... probably 90% of all the 78s that Ellington ever made and through that experience that Ben Webster was probably for me the loveliest tenor saxophonist that ever lived.

R.D.R.: How important was Ellington music to you?

C.T.: Well... it's... the... it is one of the foundations of the music that I play. It ranks with the greatest music I ever heard.

R.D.R.: Did you know him personally?

C.T.: No, my mother grew up in an area that had Count Basie and Sonny Greer.

R.D.R.: New Jersey?

C.T.: Yeah... the Ellington lore, L-O-R-E was what I grew up with. I rather resisted it till I was about 15 or 16.

R.D.R.: In favor of what?

C.T.: Oh a lot of people, I liked Cab Calloway and Chick Webb and Jimmy Lunceford. Glenn Miller and Tommy Dorsey. It

[3] Andrew Cyrille has been one of Cecil Taylor's regular drummers.

wasn't until I got involved with Charlie Barnet that the next step was Ellington. "Redskin Rhumba" was my favorite. Also the sound of that band (Barnet's) was different from even the Woody Herman band.

R.D.R.: It almost had a territory feel and sound to it.

C.T.: Yeah, I would say it had a different kind of intonation.

R.D.R.: What was your first professional gig?

C.T.: I don't remember. The first time I played with musicians was in Flushing High School. The tune that we played was a tune called "Confessin'."

R.D.R.: Jazz?

C.T.: Of course that's what we were thinking we were doing.

R.D.R.: I thought perhaps it was do-wop crooning.

C.T.: I did go through a period in the early '50s when I'd sing on dates. I do that now too.

R.D.R.: Wordless vocals.

C.T.: Yeah.

R.D.R.: You played with Johnny Hodges, Lawrence Brown, Lips Page.

C.T.: But there's one name you should have down there that you don't have. A trumpeter named McCoy or just Coy. He was living in Harlem at the time (early '50s) and that was a series of jobs that I really... that may have been more informative than any other jobs.... Ah, he would never hire a bass player and he would play at such god awful tempos, I mean he would play at the fastest tempos and he would....The realm of his playing demanded that the piano left hand would speak and so, as he was pausing, he would lean over and say, "Boy where is your left hand?" I think I must have worked with him on and off weekends for about a year.

R.D.R.: How long did you play with Lips Page?

C.T.: Oh, I don't think it was very long. I think Hot Lips liked me... I mean I'm a very well brought up... ah... disposed or displaced peasant of the Black middle class... I've always been mannerly, I mean that's part of the way I was brought up, and the involvement of music, which of course since my mother played piano and spoke three languages and did some acting and wrote poetry. And her only brother played violin, drums and piano... I mean he's the key in a certain way... he'd go to Harlem and stay for a day or two and dressed very beautifully, gave me my first drum lesson, I remember him playing stride piano. His name was William Raglin.

R.D.R.: Was there anybody you tried to model your piano playing...

C.T.: Oh, I've always been a sponge for the people I felt were great.

R.D.R.: Which includes?

C.T.: Ah... well... it includes a lot of people, ranges from Jelly Roll Morton... ah, the last really important influence in my playing would be Horace (Silver) and (Thelonious) Monk. The one continual influence in my playing would be Monk... Ellington of course... Ellington of course... Bud Powell... I think the early Erroll Garner thing. But I discovered very early that it wasn't quite enough for me to imitate people, mostly because, and that relates back to this Mary Lou Williams business 'cause the thing that people usually don't understand is... you must surrender whatever preconceptions you have about music if you're really interested in it. So that leads you to understand the really poetic essence of that music. And what I'm talking about is the spirit that informs those people as to what the music should be made of. It wasn't about imitating the notes that Bud Powell played or Erroll Garner or Jelly Roll, it was understanding the passion that informs. It's about the culture.

R.D.R.: Back in the '50s-'60s there was much more sniping at your music from fellow musicians and critics—kind of sensationalist headline copy—such as some name musician being quoted as saying about your music, "He ain't playin' shit," or some such barbs. What was the effect of that on you?

C.T.: Well, fortunately being in New York one gets tough. In order to survive in New York you have to understand what it is you want to do and then you simply deal.

R.D.R.: What was the effect for or on you of the publishing of *Four Lives in the Bebop Business* ?[4]

C.T.: None that I can see... see, what people don't understand is that for all the maybe noble thoughts that the author of that book might have had... ah, that author was at that time trying to make his way as a major writer. He was also under the very strong influences of LeRoi Jones[5]—so that essentially when he interviewed me my feeling is that he never really saw me at all... and the information he obtained was of a particular kind. You can't separate... a person's being most privately from what it is they're saying they're doing.

R.D.R.: How long since you have held a non-musical job?

C.T.: Since 1962... but that doesn't tell the whole story since I've been on welfare since '62.

R.D.R.: How long has music been your total financial support?

C.T.: I suppose since '67.

[4] *Four Lives in the Bebop Business,* by A.B. Spellman, published in 1966 by Random House, was the first book to deal seriously and in depth with musicians (Ornette Coleman, Herbie Nichols, Jackie McLean, Cecil Taylor) who, for the most part, were directly involved with post-Bop, so called Free Music.

[5] LeRoi Jones, aka Amiri Baraka, an American poet and playwright who has been involved in various revolutionary and Black identity movements since the '50s. During the New Music movement of the '60s he was active as a critic and advancing the idea of art, avant-garde art in particular, as political statement and sociological reflection.

R.D.R.: What do you do when you are not playing?

C.T.: Live, reading, dancing, going to the theatre, things like that.

R.D.R.: Do you practice a lot?

C.T.: I don't think I practice a lot, I think I practice enough to be comfortable.

R.D.R.: Do you sleep in pajamas?

C.T.: Ah, I don't sleep in pajamas... I don't sleep very much actually... I watch basketball games... I used to be a basketball player when I was young.

R.D.R.: Aren't you considered kind of short to be a basketball player?

C.T.: Yes, but when I was a basketball player I was probably the most aggressive basketball player.... I was fast.

R.D.R.: Play dirty?

C.T.: Ah... I was not foolish since everybody was a lot larger than I was.... I took advantage of my size so certain people humored me... but I made my share of baskets.

R.D.R.: How important is living in Manhattan to you?

C.T.: Oh, it used to be a lot more important than it is now. I don't have to live in New York now at all. I am of course aware that in order to do what I want to do does not only concern me. I would like very much to leave Manhattan but I would also like the band to leave. Maybe in another year if we get enough work we can, I could do it now.

R.D.R.: How important is the group and Jimmy Lyons in particular to Cecil Taylor music?

C.T.: Oh, Jimmy Lyons is the right arm of Cecil Taylor's music. He's the instructor.

R.D.R.: Is there anything else you'd like to say?

C.T.: (Chuckles) Like down with the press?

R.D.R.: If you wish. Do you feel a pressure to constantly be fresh and new in music?

C.T.: I don't think about that. The nice thing about, say, if you work over a week's period, you can see the difference at the end of a week. . . . And . . . you have to prepare yourself to do that. That's why I think living is so important.

Sun Ra

Sun Ra (aka Sonny Blount and Le Sony'r Ra) is believed to have been born around 1915. On this subject and most others concerning his early background he is circuitously vague—suggesting that he arrived on earth from another world. In the mid-'50s he began working in experimental music, his main vehicle of exploration being his Solar Arkestra. The band, which was based in Chicago in the '50s, in New York City in the '60s, and since the '70s in Philadelphia, is made up of a variety of musicians of various proficiencies, all of whom generally accept the paternal guidance of Sun Ra. This guidance ranges from simple musical direction to personal consultation. For some, this consultation entails what most would consider merely normal everyday decisions. Beyond the trappings of his rather bizarre persona Sun Ra has been involved in the vanguard of New Music since the '50s and has documented his music on over 100 LP records (many of them produced on his own El Saturn label).

Seer or charlatan, Sun Ra had developed a loyal following and managed to survive the various shifts of Jazz tastes by being always outside of any mainstream of direction.

I interviewed Sun Ra in Philadelphia in August 1977, in the apartment of Spencer Weston, a man who helped Mr. Ra in various capacities and who, at the time, was a reviewer for *Cadence*.

R.D.R.: There is a vagueness about your career before joining up with Fletcher Henderson in Chicago in the late '40s. Perhaps we could go back to some of your earliest memories.

S.R.: Well, actually the vagueness comes from the fact I never been part of the planet, I've been isolated from a child away from it. Right in the midst of everything and not being a part of it. Them troubles people got, prejudices and all that, I didn't know a thing about it, til I got to be about 14 years old. It was as if I was somewhere else that imprinted this purity on my mind, another kind of world. That is my music playing the kind of world I know about. It's like someone else from another planet trying to find out what to do. That's the kind of mind or spirit I have, it's not programmed—from the family, from the church, from the schools, from the government. I don't have a programmed mind. I know about what they're talking about, but they don't know about what I'm talking about. I'm in the midst of what they're doing but they've never been in the midst of what has been impressed upon my mind as being a pure solar world. I started to put in the music what I know is going to be the future of humanity. I've always played about space. Particularly like in Chicago, the first song I was using as a theme song, "New Horizons."

R.D.R.: When was this?

S.R.: I don't know the years. I wasn't in a time zone. I wasn't part of my so-called generation. It was about maybe a year before he (Fletcher Henderson) died. It must have been about '49 or '50.

Now I played with Stuff Smith and Coleman Hawkins on the north side of Chicago. I played with Wynonie Harris too, at one time for three or four months in Nashville, Tennessee, at a club there.

R.D.R.: Before Fletcher Henderson?

S.R.: Right... I also played with Lil Greene, too. I played with her band off and on. I played with Jesse Miller, too. He was a top trumpet man.

R.D.R.: Did you record with any of these people?

S.R.: I did one with Wynonie Harris. I don't think it reached up here. You know they make a lot of records in the south that don't reach up here. It was a white company, it might have been a race label—I don't even know the name of it. It was 'bout five or six pieces.

R.D.R.: And you recorded with Stuff Smith.

S.R.: It's the most beautiful thing you ever heard. It happens to be made at my house.

R.D.R.: Who were the first people you played with?

S.R.: Well, I played with Paul Bascomb, he had a band. I was sort of affiliated with Erskine Hawkins since a lot of my friends were in there like Dick Bascomb. This was around Montgomery, Alabama. That's where Erskine Hawkins' headquarters was.

R.D.R.: It's been listed that you toured with Fess Whatley.

S.R.: I didn't ever tour with him, he's a friend of mine; when we were on the East Coast, from Florida on up, we were touring that and he sponsored that. He bought the bus and everything. We had just gotten out of high school.

R.D.R.: Was it a territory band?

S.R.: Not really. We just between high school and college. In fact all of us went to college together.

R.D.R.: Was that around 1934?

S.R.: No, that's not true because I played with the band all through high school because that was a teachers' band. Nobody in it but school teachers with degrees. I played with it because I was only somebody could sight read; he had a huge repertoire. It was like a sax-o-society band because they only play for exclusive people. Mostly only played for White people in exclusive places and social clubs where the Black people at. Black society and White society. They played everything, that's the reason I know about standards because he had everything all the way back to the stomp, Dixieland. We played everything.

R.D.R.: That was your first formal musical experience?

S.R.: No, I was playing with another band. I played with a band called Society Troubadours. See, I was in society then. They too played for social clubs mostly. They didn't have a leader except sometimes Fred Averytt (I think that's his name, I don't know how to spell it). He organized it at first, then it came a time I was arranger for them, but before that I was playing with another band, with my school mates, they had a band too. We always be going outside of the city (Birmingham, Ala.) every summer playing. I never did stay in one place.

R.D.R.: How did you get into music?

S.R.: They teach the public school music, but I wasn't thinking about being in music 'cause I had read about poets and writers and wise men all having a difficult time as human beings, so I didn't intend to get in that. But one day I came home; maybe I was ten years old, and then I had a piano there waiting for me as a present. The opposition came from my grandmother who always said musicians always die young, they be sickly. She opposed it. Then I sat down at the piano and played it, which was astounding 'cause I had never played the piano. They thought I was playing by ear, even though I was reading it. I played everything they put up there.

R.D.R.: Was that your first instrument?

S.R.: I believe it was a kazoo, or maybe it was blowing through a comb, I believe I did when I was about six years old.

R.D.R.: What did your parents do?

S.R.: Well, I had some different kind of parents. They say you make your own Heaven and Hell, they don't go to church. Always taught me to treat everyone right, not to abuse anyone. They always saw to me knowing about life.

At nine years old I went to see a sex movie about the results of sex when people had disease. I saw that. At ten I was (with) a secret organization—American Woodman. They showed me discipline, you have to march. I learned all about secret orders, discipline, how to be a leader from 10 to 14 or 15.

R.D.R.: Did your parents have occupations?

S.R.: They had restaurants.

R.D.R.: How about your grandmother?

S.R.: Well, mostly she was in church, all during the week that's all she did—except the time she tried to get me to go. (She said) it was all right to play the church songs.

R.D.R.: You have been vague about your birth date but your work with Fess Whatley would seem to mark it about 1914-15.

S.R.: Well, I don't talk too much about the dates because of the controversial aspects. I arrived on this planet on a very important day, it's been pinpointed by wisemen, astrologers as a very important date. I arrived at the exact moment a very controversial arrival, so that's the only reason I don't talk about it.

R.D.R.: What makes it controversial?

S.R.: Well, it's the way the stars were set at that moment. In a position where a spiritual being can arrive right at that particular point.

R.D.R.: Do you see your arrival as some sort of messiah?

S.R.: No, because I've been taught from other planes of existence, that the best hope for man is destruction. You wouldn't save a rotten apple. They look at man as not worth saving.

R.D.R.: How do you see humanity?

S.R.: Well, they don't have any discipline. They always talking about freedom but they don't demonstrate they're free 'cause they bow to death all the time. Since they do die they are not free. On the other hand I've been taught some things that humanity knows nothing about whatsoever. I don't talk too much about it 'cause people get in an uproar, in a frenzy. Anybody else can say anything; when I say it, it strikes them some kind of way. I'm trying to figure that out as to why.

R.D.R.: Do you see yourself as free?

S.R.: I'm a free spirit. I see myself as P-H-R-E but not F-R-E-E. That's the name of the sun in ancient Egypt. I'm not really a person at all... immortal spirit. I'm not part of this. I'm just a test for humanity as whether they can accept something that's different. They talk about freedom. Can they give somebody freedom that's different? Can they tolerate other types of beings? They've got this government of the people, by the people and for the people. They didn't include me, I'm a leader, I'm not the people. Leaders are supposed to be assassinated and used by the people.

R.D.R.: You've led a band and, like Ellington and Basie, had loyal associations with many of its members.

S.R.: The people stay with them because they're making money. In my case they didn't stay with me because of money. Actually this organization wasn't about religion, wasn't really about loyalty, it wasn't about anything, that's what make it an unusual organization; 'cause they didn't have no ulterior motives. I'm a leader in the sense I've been able to coordinate some people together, each one of them a totally different personality.

R.D.R.: You haven't been assassinated?

S.R.: Well, they assassinate me with words in magazines and things. You don't have to shoot nobody to assassinate them, you can do it with words. Words hurt too, you know... they do. I ain't been no leader in a physical sense, they assassinate those kind, so in that way I'm not a leader.

I'm a scientist, I deal with equations. You might say a spiritual scientist and also a cosmo musical scientist. I know all kinds of things about music which people have been talking about doing, but I can do it. Like if I had a symphony orchestra to work with, I can do all sorts of things that they can't even dream can be done with instruments, 'cause I got all the answers from the cosmos. But I have to have the musicians to work with, I have to have the instruments to work with. This would call for strict discipline to play this music the way it's supposed to be played. This planet got to produce a master musician, a world musician, before it be reorganized by the cosmos.

R.D.R.: How do we recognize one?

S.R.: A world musician can go in any country and tailor-make it up from the traditional up to the future where the whole nation can move forward. He would know them if he went to China he would know all about Chinese, he would know what they need. He would know it in Egypt. If every nation were moved up to a certain point in music you'd have harmony among the nations. But you got one nation way back at 1500 and one at 1000 and one way back in the Stone Age; you can't never have no get together because they in a different time zone. That's what's happening on this planet, each nation is in a different time zone. This America you might call in limbo, that's what makes it potential, it has a possibility of doing something with music. No, some people try to bypass Jazz and they did America a great disservice, they almost destroy the country doing that. There are some more people realize that they should let this music represent America but the American people two generations gone by and they don't know anything about it, where in Europe they do. This is a planned strategy by people to bypass particular Black musicians that were the masters. And to put some more Black musicians up there who are imitators. They put the imitators up there instead of the creators.

R.D.R.: Who do you feel are the creators?

S.R.: Well, Duke Ellington was a creator, Fletcher Henderson, too. Fats Waller was a creator, too. I really can't think of any more. A lot of musicians put up on top that have photographic minds, you would call that a creator, I'm not talking about that kind. All the time I was growing up I saw the creators being bypassed. And that's the reason I determined to have a band so, well, that's not going to happen like that. That's the reason I've taken a lot of hardships to insist on people recognizing creative masters as well as other people.

They destroyed the big bands through raiding it and taking the stars out, giving them a trio or a quartet or something like that. As a result, you destroy initiative and cause total chaos and confusion of the people in the Black communities.

Music is a universal language and most certainly could be a national language to communicate to different nations. A band can demonstrate unity among men more than anything else in the world.

R.D.R.: There seems to be some confusion about your name. When you were playing in high school, what were you called?

S.R.: Sunny. But my name wasn't Blount you know. They say that. All you have to do is go to the Library of Congress and look and see what they say.

R.D.R.: What was your name?

S.R.: Well, that's a secret. It was Sunny, but it wasn't Sunny Blount though. My real name is Le Sony'r Ra. It's (Blount) not a bad name; it wasn't no good name for me, it didn't have no rhythm.

One time I called myself, before I used the name Blount, Sunny Lee. But I changed that because you had a Baron Lee out there and also since Lee lost the Civil War. I knew that the name Ra was really my name anyway.

R.D.R.: Was Ra the last name of your parents?

S.R.: It was Arman. It comes from ancient Egypt.

R.D.R.: How did the Blount name come about?

S.R.: Because I had some relatives named that. I used it sometimes when I copyrighted, but I spelled it Bhlount.

R.D.R.: Why?

S.R.: Well, that's the way Fletcher Henderson did. He would be doing some things under another name. Like on this pop record that became popular, "Batman" (theme), I'm playing the organ on that. I'm playing the record on the one that became a hit.

R.D.R.: How did that come about?

S.R.: Well, I had a friend in New York City and we were there and we needed some money. John (Gilmore) is on that, Marshall's (Allen) on that. We did a lot of that, sometimes I didn't even know the names of the songs or the record company. I didn't really care, I needed some money to keep from starving. They knew we could read anything, so the arrangers always like us to come and we back them. It was just a recording session, going to make such and such amount, that's all we concerned with. It didn't make any difference, you just read. Some records they never did release. We made a record with Chief Bey on MGM. They never did put it out—that was a very nice record.

R.D.R.: You've recorded for numerous record companies, were you ever under exclusive contract with them?

S.R.: Well, I didn't really intend for this music to get out to the general public. It was just for the creator of the universe.

(Sun Ra went on to explain that much of what he considers his best music he has held back from commercial release.)

R.D.R.: What's the purpose of holding music back?

S.R.: Because somebody was trying to keep the music from being heard. So I wasn't going to go out there.

R.D.R.: But that someone seems to be you in this case.

S.R.: Well, I mean they were doing it, so I just fought fire with fire. They didn't want me to be heard, so I said okay. So I went on and I studied me some more stuff and it gave me time to really develop myself mentally and spiritually. I did resist 'cause if I hadn't resisted them they would have turned around and given it to one of their pets and they be out there playing it. So therefore I didn't put my stuff (music) out there, I put me some more stuff out there for them to steal. So they stole that and now I can put my other stuff out there and the public can hear what I'm really doing now. I think it's a good strategy.

R.D.R.: It would seem you make it easy to suppress your music.

S.R.: No, I just gave them a false impression. They were trying to deceive me, so I deceived them. And they will know how much they missed in the last 20 years. I just wanted to play my music and they should have paid me. Like even now, like Impulse and the rest of them. I finally made some for them 'cause I didn't want people to feel I'm trying to have a monopoly on music. So I finally consented to make some for them (Impulse) and what did they do? They cut the ends off so I don't get any royalties. Impulse was going to spend almost a million dollars in publicity. They were going to put out 14 LPs at one time. Something happened where they didn't keep their contract.

When I put the real music out there (on Saturn) then the people can see.

R.D.R.: How about the Improvising Artist material, is that you?

S.R.: Well, they won't be able to steal that 'cause there are some nuances on the piano that every piano player can't get. Like Richard Abrams said, you got the brilliant touch. But like I say, when I put these things out there, the world will understand. It's out there but you can't find it on the commercial (labels). Like the Montreux ('76) Festival, they wanted to buy it outright, $3000.

R.D.R.: Who?

S.R.: Since I didn't talk with them personally I'd better not say. They sent it through somebody else. Some of the companies that have offered some things have been Muse, Inner City, but they haven't come out with any prices.

R.D.R.: There is one thing on Inner City Records, a French recording.

S.R.: Yeah, they got that from a company over there. That wasn't supposed to be released in this country. I didn't make it for America, I made it for the French.

R.D.R.: What would it take for you to record for a company.

S.R.: It would probably take $100,000 in the first place. I'd have to be sure the studio is the proper kind of studio to catch the band.

R.D.R.: It seems success on those terms will be hard to find at this time.

S.R.: I did never want to be successful. I want to be the only thing I could be without anybody stopping me in America—that is, to be a failure. So I feel pretty good about it, I'm a total failure. Nobody can stop you from being a failure. (Laughter.)

So now as I've been successful as a failure, I can be successful.

R.D.R.: So you really have no gripes. . .

S.R.: Of course I don't. I want to thank them because at the time they made me a failure I was able to study and now I know everything.

R.D.R.: What are you trying to achieve now? What is your purpose?

S.R.: Well. . . I suppose, to stay out. I'm not trying to really achieve anything. I can't be going out there presenting in that world 'cause that world's not mine. I'm talking about something from other planes of existence. These people on this planet only understand life and death. If you talk about something outside of that they don't even have no cognition of it whatsoever. They be meditating, I told them why don't you cogitate. Talk about teaching people, I'd have to close all the schools and start all over.

America realize the value of Jazz now. But unfortunately the masters that are really playing it are all gone. To bridge this generation gap they got a problem, I'm the only somebody that can do it. You might say I'm the spirit of Jazz. I know all forms of Jazz. I know how to take a band and to create, that's 'cause of the experience I had as a child with a band. I wasn't out there in the combo thing. That's the reason it never interested me in solo piano and that. Somebody start out with combos and trios and solos. The bigger the band the better. I'm always talking to musicians, let's get a 2000 piece band and they can't conceive of that. Now that interests me. But you know if you go out and tell musicians that—strange enough, they shake their heads astounded. I tell 'em you in the harmony department, out of all the men on Earth you should be delighted to get together to demonstrate harmony. If you demonstrate harmony, then the rest of the men in other sections of life can see that harmony can be demonstrated. I'm dealing with the truth. I know exactly how to color music in such a way I need maybe two or three thousand pieces to interest me.

R.D.R.: Have you tried to apply for grants for such a project?

S.R.: No, because they don't offer enough money to do what I have to do. Them little pittance they give like 3000, 5000 dollars, I spend that on one instrument. Willis Conover was talking one day and he said, well, he offered me grants of $50,000. A friend of mine standing there said that's ridiculous. Said, how much do you want? He said, "Want a million dollars for every state in the union. We want a concert hall set up in each state so they can hear this music properly," and $1,000,000 from each state is not too much to ask for a cultural hall.

R.D.R.: What did he say?

S.R.: Well, he just stood there and said, "Are you kidding?" He said "No, this music is worth millions of dollars and it's for the welfare of this country. Russia's looking for a world music, Sun Ra's got the world music so it ain't no more than right that he should have something to work with."

But I'm dealing with world music, now where am I going to get money unless I go to the U.N.? They don't have no money either. Maybe I can go to the World Bank as a government. If I declare myself as a government, which I'm thinking about doing, then I could go to the World Bank and get me some money.

Milt Hinton

Milt Hinton was the bassist for the Cab Calloway band from 1936 through the early '50s. Since then he has free-lanced around the New York area, including stays with Louis Armstrong and Benny Goodman, among others, as well as with various studio orchestras. His skill, engaging spirit, and adaptable technique have made him one of the most called-for bassists in Jazz.

I had arranged to interview Mr. Hinton during his stay in Potsdam, New York. Unfortunately, conflicting schedules made it impossible to manage any decent block of time in which to do an interview. Finally, we agreed to meet at the Massena New York airport prior to Mr. Hinton's flight home. It was a windy, cold April 1978 day, and since the airport afforded no privacy we retreated to my subcompact car to do the interview. Mr. Hinton both as a bassist and conversationalist is open and outgoing. Quite simply he was the easiest interview I have yet conducted.

R.D.R.: You were born in Vicksburg...

M.H.: Yeah, Vicksburg, Mississippi; June 23, 1910.

R.D.R.: Were you exposed to any of the area Blues?

M.H.: I didn't realize it as Blues; my first recollections of music is hearing these guys late at night, strollers, as we called them. A bass violin and maybe a guitar and clarinet, and they would be playin' very softly. People would get up at 11, 12 o'clock at night, give them nickels and dimes and this is the way they made their little wine money. And this is the formal Jazz type of thing that I have recollections of. Most of my background was church music and popular music. There was a piano in the house. My mother was an organist of Mt. Heridon Baptist Church there. So I grew up in the church and our house was like a center for choir rehearsals.

Most of the Black people were trying to migrate out of there. My first uncle left there in 1910 'cause he had heard about the good things that were happening in Chicago—everybody was following the river—they heard there was work to be had. They had to find manual labor, and the Chicago stockyards could afford that. Also, Chicago at that time was the center of the U.S.A., and so there were heads of hotels there, and where they have hotels they got to have porters and bellhops. Bellhops can make a fantastic amount of money even in 1910-15, my uncle says they could make $50 a day. If you got into the right hotel and the right connections, and then into the prostitution thing—always you have guy's check in says he wants to know if there's a good girl around. The girls are working the hotel in cooperation with the bellhops, see—you give me a good john I give you a good tip; the guy says you give me a good girl I give you a tip. So he makes a tip both ways.

R.D.R.: Like a stockbroker.

M.H.: Sure, and then as soon as they get together first thing they want a little drink and he (the bellhop) just made him a tub full of gin downstairs in the basement and he sells him that for five bucks and the guy's got it pretty well made. So it took from 1910 to about 1917 for my uncle to send for another brother and another sister, another sister, till they accumulated enough family there and they set up housekeeping, rented a nice apartment and furnished it and sent for my grandmother and me and my mother's youngest sister. I guess it was 1917 when we finally got to Chicago. My mother and father separated when I was three months old and I was raised without a father—I never saw my father till I was 30. But my mother's family was so beautiful to me.

R.D.R.: You talked about these strollers, back in Vicksburg, was that like string band music?

M.H.: They just walked the street like a hustle. They had the same kind of musical influence as new releases.

R.D.R.: Street musicians?

M.H.: Street musicians!

R.D.R.: Playing popular music of the day?

M.H.: Playing popular music of the day.

R.D.R.: Improvising?

M.H.: Improvising... a little singin'. One guy, named One Eye Mace, he was a bass player from New Orleans. They drank wine—the hustle scene. I never saw that deep Mississippi Blues, I was never involved in that. My musical background came from the time I was 13 or 14 and delivering newspapers. The scene was fabulous, Chicago was a hotbed by that time, all the great musicians, Freddie Keppard, Louis Armstrong, King Oliver, Jelly Roll Morton was coming through, Ethel Waters was playing at the Royal Garden Cafe, Erskine Tate had this fantastic band at the Vendome Theatre. There was Eddie South, Tommy Weatherford, Earl Hines, Barney Bigard all in these bands. These were my idols, seeing all of these guys. In the morning I see the waiters picking up tables and these guys in tuxedos and I'm saying, "My god, I got to get into that way."

R.D.R.: Was there an early idol for you?

M.H.: Quinn Wilson was the idol for most of us, being a day or two older than I. He was the one in Wendell Phillips High School that I saw. He was Captain in ROTC, he played violin in the orchestra, he played bass, he played piano, very talented and I always wanted to do—when he graduated from high school I was lucky enough to get the first chair to the violin and when I graduated I handed that first chair over to Ray Nance. You hear so much talk about the Austin High gang, you never hear anything about the Wendell Phillips gang. This high school, we had so many great musicians that came out of there. There was Lionel Hampton, Nat Cole, Eddie Cole, Urbie Gage, Ray Nance...

R.D.R.: Kind of like DuSable High School.[1]

M.H.: Oh, that's a later era. I graduated from Wendell Phillips in 1929 and they were building DuSable. At Wendell Phillips we had Major Clark Smith as our musical director. So the musical life has always been there.

R.D.R.: Who was the greatest influence on your musical concepts?

M.H.: My mother, which was why I can't play piano to this day, because my mother taught piano. Nat Cole was one of the kids coming by. I resented being told to go to bed or take a piano lesson. My mother says I didn't cotton to it so she sent me to a violin teacher, Professor James Johnson. He was a magnificent man, a most lovable man and I just fell in love with him and wanted to study. This was around 1925. I got a scholarship with him. Then I got into the school brass band, so I could travel and go on trips. That's where I got with the tuba. I'm a very sad tuba player. My very first recording in 1930 with Tiny Parham and I'm playin' tuba on this record. If you want to know why I'm playing bass now, just listen to that record. It's just ridiculous.

R.D.R.: That's how you got into the bass?

M.H.: That's how, and I found I really love those big instruments. At this time tuba was just fading out of the bands, converting to bass violins and the drummers didn't really like this, they missed that stiff tuba sound. There was a great bass player named Bill Johnson in Chicago, he just died at almost 100

[1]DuSable High School is a public school in Chicago through which an inordinate number of top Jazz artists have passed. Its music department was headed by Capt. Walter Dyett. See the Von Freeman interview.

years old. He was a great player, big red-faced man, New Orleans-Creole gentleman. He used to say "jump a hair" when he played... "Hey, baby, jump a hair." He had that bass going. The next great bass player that I heard was Wellman Braud, with Duke Ellington; he was a dignified Creole gentleman. I'd just sit and listen to that band and watch him play that stomp two beat on "Ring Them Bells." I'd wish he'd just drop his bow or resin so I could hand it to him. I finally found out his sister lived right next door to my mother and I waited till she got to her garbage so I could ask her could I come in to say hello to her brother. And we got to be dear friends as the years went by.

R.D.R.: Which bassist do you think did the most to liberate the bass from its tuba functioning?

M.H.: Well, I came into the thing with two beats and then it began to go into four beats. Braud[2] began to do four-beat things, he was to my idea *the* bass player, of course Pops Foster[3] was doing the slap bass thing. The next influence to really revolutionize bass was, of course, Jimmy Blanton.[4] I was with the Cab Calloway band then. Jimmy came into the scene and revolutionized with the solo type of bass playing.

R.D.R.: Had you wanted to play with Duke's band?

M.H.: No, not really, I was established with Cab's band. That was just as much a great band as Ellington's in that era from the musicians inside. In fact, Cab Calloway paid more money than Duke Ellington at that time, so I had made the epitome of band business.

R.D.R.: What's the story of Ellington getting Ben Webster?

M.H.: Well, Cab and Duke worked out of the same office, they were brother bands and they were dear friends. Ben Webster

[2]Wellman Braud (1891-1966) was Duke Ellington's bassist from 1926-1935.

[3]George "Pops" Foster (1892-1969), one of the first great bassists; born in New Orleans he spent many years with Louis Armstrong and was active in music until the end of his life.

[4]Jimmy Blanton (1921-1942) was Duke Ellington's bassist in the late '30s and is credited with opening up the role of Jazz bass as a solo instrument beyond its merely rhythmic function.

was in Cab Calloway's band and, being a great soloist and a great player, he always wanted to play with Duke. But there was no way. He would make his desires known that he wanted to play with Duke, and Duke being the very clever man that he was, told Ben, "I would love to have you in the band, but Cab's is my brother band and I can't take anybody out of his band. *But,* if you didn't have a job I'd have to give you one." This started the chemistry in Ben and he started saving up his money and about six months later we hit Cleveland, Ohio, and Fletcher Henderson's band was at the Grand Terrace at Chicago and Duke was going to play the Jeffrey Tavern in Chicago—so Ben put in his notice with Cab. Cab was very distraught about it, said, "Look, I need a good tenor player." Cab was payin' good money, wanted to raise Ben's salary—we had no soloists for Ben, Cab was a soloist. He said, "Can you get me a good player?" So Ben said, "Sure, I think I can get you Chu Berry." He was with Fletcher Henderson, who was paying $25 a week, and Cab is paying $35 a week, so there was no trouble. So Chu came over to Cleveland and then Ben Webster and Chu Berry sat side by side and Ben showed him the book and then Ben left and went to Chicago with no job. He went on the corners and told Duke "Well, I'm unemployed." And Duke hired him.

R.D.R.: Tell us something about the Cassino Simpson Band.

M.H.: We called him Cas Simpson.

R.D.R.: It never recorded?

M.H.: Well, there are some records. They were made while he was in an insane asylum, which was absolutely illegal. A pianist of that era named Zinky Cohn, a Black guy and an official of the union, he was able to go into the insane asylum and make some tapes. I've never heard them.

Well, about Cas Simpson, he played piano, a very fine pianist. I remember him coming in from Milwaukee but I never really knew where Cas was from. He was a very stout, stocky, very fair complected Black man with pockmarks on his face. He smoked a cigar, always had it in his mouth and chewed it—spitting all around himself on the floor, but he was an *insane* piano player.

He played just incessantly, and fantastic things. I think only Art Tatum would have outpulled him. My first meeting was at this club in Chicago. Louis Armstrong was makin' his first trip east with a band. It was a trumpet room and they wanted some trumpet player to follow Louis in the room. They sent to Milwaukee and they got Jabbo Smith and made him the leader. They hired me for bass, Orthello Chesleigh was the guitar and banjo player, Cas was the piano player, Floyd Campbell was the drummer, Jerome Pasquel was the very fine lead alto man, a fellow named John Thomas played trombone, Ed Burke played trombone. Well, Jabbo was kind of a tardy type of guy at that time, he didn't come, came late for a gig, so Cas would take over and do the soloing and playing. So the next season instead of hiring Jabbo back, he hired Cas as the band leader.

R.D.R.: This was around 1930?

M.H.: Yeah, he must have been 30 then also. He lost his mind. I don't know when he died. But this was a band that really made it big in Chicago. We were all together.

R.D.R.: How come it never recorded?

M.H.: I don't know, we played the Regal and I have pictures of the band. I don't know. But he wrote a lot of original arrangements and the other thing Cas wrote was about food: "Chitlins and Rice," "Greens and Bacon" and "Fatback and Molasses" some of his tunes were, if I remember, and they were swinging tunes. But it was a shortlived band, didn't last but maybe one season, five, maybe six months at this particular club. Then the guy who owned the club started to form the Three Deuces and I went in there with Zutty Singleton (drummer).

R.D.R.: You were also part of the New York Bass Violin Choir in the '60s.

M.H.: That was one of the delights of my life, to be affiliated with what I consider some of the finest bass players in the world. Bill Lee organized this group as an opening for some of his works, and he's an excellent bassist, great musician and tremendous arranger and he has just a natural great talent.

Anyway, it was a job to work with Bill and Ron Carter, Richard Davis, Lisle Atkinson, Michael Fleming, Sam Jones. We were all busy in New York and we would get up at 9 o'clock in the morning, meet at Richard Davis' house and practice till one of us had a date.

We have some tapes of it, but we never decided what to do with it.

R.D.R.: Before the interview you mentioned Joe Venuti. There's a story about him and bass players in Chicago. True?

M.H.: Yeah, but it wasn't Chicago. It was in Hollywood, California. And it was tuba players. He went through the union book and called up all these tuba players and told them he had a gig for them and to be at Sunset and Vine and he sat around watched all them guys show up. Of course the union took it to him and made him pay for it; it was a great joke and he paid for it. But when he played Chicago, about 26 bass players decided to show up for fun. So that's how that story got out, but they planned it for a little publicity stunt. He bought all the guys a drink and bought them a double so it cost him a couple of hundred bucks for that. He's a delightful man and the guru of the music business as far as I'm concerned. A great human being, artist, I just can't think of anything but superlatives for Joe Venuti.

R.D.R.: In his autobiography, Cab Calloway says you were the spitball thrower, not Dizzy Gillespie—true?

M.H.: No, that isn't true. He said that in the book but that isn't so. The spitball was thrown and it landed beside me. It was a Sunday afternoon on the stage of the Hartford (Conn.) Theatre and we had a spot in the show called The Cab Jivers—Tyree Glenn, Chu Berry, Danny Barker, Cozy Cole and myself. We'd go out and do a couple of tunes and the lights would go down on the band. Dizzy had taught me a tune, "Girl of My Dreams," and he taught me a bass solo and he had used some flatted fifths in there and it wasn't sittin' too good with my ear and I couldn't hear it and nine tunes out of ten I missed it. Everytime I played it I'd look back at Dizzy and if I made it Dizzy would signal cool with open fingers and if I missed it, he would stick his finger in one nostril and wave his hand with the other and say you stink. Well this Sunday afternoon when I went to play this thing, I missed it a mile. I looked back at Dizzy and Dizzy waved his hand and gestured you stink. At that moment, another musician, who shall remain nameless, right between his legs he thumped a big wad of paper right up in the air and it landed in the spotlight right beside me on the stage. And Cab Calloway's in the wings with two beautiful ladies and his white suit and he sees this piece of paper go down and Dizzy with his finger to his nose and his hand waving. When the show was over and the band walked off, he lit into Dizzy and bawled the daylights out of him. He was always doing something wrong, so he was deserving of it in the respect if anything was wrong, it was always Dizzy; that's the reason we called him Dizzy. Cab says, "You idiot, these guys are performing on the stage and you're acting like a kid out there throwing spitballs." Dizzy says, "Fess," that's what we called him, for Professor. "Fess, I didn't do it." Cab says, "You're a damned liar, you did do it, I'm looking right at you when you threw it." Now this is the first time Dizzy is right in his whole life and he says, "You're another damned liar, I didn't do it." Cab has these two beautiful ladies next to him and he didn't want to be insulted, especially by the youngest guy in the band. So he hauls off and slaps Dizzy upside the head and when he did that Dizzy came up with a knife and he really was going to lay it into him. I happen to be standing there and I just happen to hit Dizzy's arm and it deflected the knife and that time Cab was able to grab Dizzy's wrist and the scuffle started and later the pachyderms, Chu Berry and Benny Payne, the big heavy guys, got there and were able to separate them 'cause I couldn't do anything with them, and push Cab into his dressing room and Diz into the band room. When Cab got in he saw the side of his white suit was all red where the knife had stuck in his leg; he had been cut. And he walked back into the dressing room and said, "Well, you know this guy has cut me," and told Diz to pack his horn and leave, and he left.

That evening when we went back to New York the bus always stopped at the Teresa Hotel, 135th and Seventh, and Cab the first one out of the bus, and there's Dizzy. He says "Fess, I'm sorry," and held out his hand and Cab hit his hand like this (slaps him five) and walked off. Of course the press played it up forever as a feud.

Cab (now) knows who did throw it, but when he wrote the book, rather than have any confrontation namin' someone that would probably contest him for that, he said I did it. But of course, I couldn't have—it doesn't make any difference. I'm sure Cab knows.[5]

R.D.R.: When you relax who do you listen to?

M.H.: When I have time I try to catch up on the records I have made and some new people, like some new bass players.

One rejuvenating force for me to go back to is always Art Tatum. I love to listen to Tatum. But I am a nut at heart, I'm a violin groupie—I think my biggest record collection is jazz violin. Having been a frustrated violin player when I was a kid, I still have that great respect for that artistry for one that plays what I consider the king of instruments.

R.D.R.: You've recorded so much and with everybody. Is there one recording you enjoy more than any?

M.H.: The "New York, New York" (with George Russell) is one I like very much.

[5]In a November 1978 interview I did with Dizzy Gillespie, Mr. Gillespie said that he and Jonah Jones went to see Cab Calloway years later and "Jonah says, 'Fess, I got a confession to make' (laughter). It was Jonah. Cab wasn't there, he was off-stage, so he didn't know who did it. But Jonah told me he did it."

Von Freeman

Von Freeman was born (10/3/22) in Chicago and has chosen to remain there. He is a graduate of DuSable High School. He has two brothers who are also active in Jazz, Bruz (drums) and George (guitar). Chicago in the '60s was an incubator for much of the New Music directions of the '70s and '80s. Some musicians give Mr. Freeman credit as being one of the teachers instrumental in that gestation. Among the many Chicago artists to become prominent in the New Wave that swept in with the '70s was Mr. Freeman's son, Chico Freeman, who, like his father, plays tenor sax.

I had lined up a series of interviews in Chicago in June 1978. Among those I specifically wished to talk with was Von Freeman. Mr. Freeman is active on the Chicago scene, and his schedule and mine were in daily conflict. Finally on the last day of my Chicago stay, we agreed to meet at 4:30 in the morning at Mr. Freeman's house after Mr. Freeman had finished playing at a local club.

R.D.R.: You have somewhat of an underground reputation?

V.F.: Yeah, that's what they call it. They call me a living legend too, whatever that means.

R.D.R.: That's another word for obscurity.

V.F.: Right... I think that's the best thing I heard about that. That's really where it is. I'm what you'd call a very popular unknown musician.

R.D.R.: Why is it?

V.F.: I don't know, it just seems to be natural. Like I'm a loner really, I think that's got a lot to do with it. I don't go any place to speak of. I don't do anything except practice; I think it's my fault more than anyone else's.

R.D.R.: But even other local Chicago artists of lesser talents were better documented in recording by the Chicago record companies like Argo/Cadet. Yet I believe you were only recorded as part of a Charlie Parker Memorial Concert, right?

V.F.: Well, I'm on a thing with Milt Trenier called "Party Time" or something for Cadet—that was in '67.

R.D.R.: But that aside, it's not much.

V.F.: Well, even today I'm not interested in recording 'less I can do what I want to do on it, so naturally most folks who record you tell you what to do and what to play. Maybe that's one of the reasons.

R.D.R.: Your Atlantic recording, was that specifically for them?

V.F.: No, Roland Kirk produced that record. He had come around me years ago and I wasn't even aware of it. And one day he called me and told me he was a great follower of mine—I couldn't believe it. He said he had been a lot of places I played but I play most times with dark glasses on and I rarely look around me. I rarely even leave bandstands, so I didn't know he was in the audience. One day he approached me and told me he liked the way I played and thought I was a very talented man—told me he was pretty set in New York and the first chance that he got he was going to record me. Well, I'd already (been) told that by several people and sure enough one day he did call and did just that.

R.D.R.: You had your way on that recording?

V.F.: Oh, yeah.

R.D.R.: What do you think of it?

V.F.: Well... I don't know. I think they (sidemen) did a beautiful job. I'd been up all night the night before for about two days and I was kind of out there. But it's generally me, facets of me, 'cause I play several different ways.

R.D.R.: I was disappointed by it. However, your Nessa recording (Nessa 6) I enjoyed immensely.

V.F.: The thing about Nessa, I was so free I almost couldn't play because Nessa demanded I do what I want to do. 'Cause with Atlantic I did write a few little pieces of music. Nessa told me to do just what I do ordinarily—I never knew how hard it was till we went to cut that record. One thing, I couldn't think of anything to play. I know hundreds of tunes. I've never been in a studio with anybody as relaxed as that man (Chuck Nessa, producer of Nessa Records). He's just interested in letting you play, he doesn't like to edit or anything. He likes your mistakes as well.

R.D.R.: But don't you think the best Jazz is imperfect?

V.F.: Oh, sure, sure, but you become so accustomed to everybody taking takes. Take 1, Take 2, Take 20, Take 40, you know.

R.D.R.: The Atlantic wasn't bad, but it didn't shake me in my boots.

V.F.: Well, someone else told me that, I think it was Marion Brown. He said he liked the Nessa album much better than the Atlantic record.

R.D.R.: Not hustling in a New York competitive scene must have its advantages.

V.F.: Well, I just kind of sit back and sort of watch the scenes. I find as far as I'm concerned personally it really has nothing to do with me. All that I deal with, I'm only as good as I play. I just played last night. If I played badly I would have been bad. All the horn players came around me, the younger guys, and if I'm playing well they say so, if I'm not they say I'm not, or just won't say anything. I'm just about as good as my last performance.

R.D.R.: You're content to remain in Chicago?

V.F.: Yeah.

R.D.R.: You haven't been tempted to move to New York?

V.F.: Oh, no... no. Oh, I've been to New York, but I'd never just move there. Well, there have been extenuating circumstances, too; it looks like I always had a few responsibilities here and I just stayed. I don't know, I haven't come up with a plausible excuse yet, but I know many fine players around here that never left here.

R.D.R.: Like John Young?

V.F.: Yeah, John Young is still here. But there are some more even older than I am. I'm 55—Oct. 3, 1922.

R.D.R.: You're another graduate of DuSable High School. What made that such a magic and special school, was it Walter Dyett?

V.F.: Oh, yeah, he made the school. The school was just a normal high school but he was a very beautiful man, very intelligent man. Very talented man and a very talented music teacher. And he made the school musical wise.

R.D.R.: It was a regular district school?

V.F.: Just a regular school.

R.D.R.: In other words, you had to be in the district to go to it.

V.F.: Right... course, everybody who was interested in music did what they could, told all kinds of stories so they could go to DuSable and study under him.

R.D.R.: Was he a Jazz artist *per se?*

V.F.: No, a disciplinarian more so than anything, I think.

R.D.R.: Did he play?

V.F.: I never did hear him play anything. While I was at DuSable I never heard Captain play anything. I think he was a Captain in the service. But, no, I never heard him play anything. He didn't really teach *per se* either; not really, like he taught saxophone but he didn't really teach saxophone—that kind of thing. It was the aura of the man, he just exuded, ah... like I still think it was discipline. He knew the fundamentals of the instruments, I would imagine, and I heard he was a violinist and a pianist, though I never heard him play either one. But he knew the basics, the fingering, the intonation of things. If you weren't correct he would tell you, that kind of thing. And he was very bent upon your reading music and studying, practicing.

R.D.R.: Was he the head of the music department?

V.F.: Yes. Then he had another thing he used to give like a musical, they called it "Hi-Jinx," and he was into a lot of different things. He had a marching band, concert, he was doing the whole thing. For a person who didn't know anything about music he was good because he would start them off correctly and stay behind you. He was really discipline.

But see, Capt. Walter Dyett had another choral teacher, her name was Mrs. Bryant Jones. And she was head of the chorus, and I went there for a while, that's really where I learned just harmony. Mrs. Bryant Jones was very good.

R.D.R.: How did you get interested in music?

V.F.: I started out on piano. This piano (living room) in fact, when I was maybe two years old. My mother is a housewife, guitarist. My father's a policeman and he played Ragtime here.

R.D.R.: Amateur?

V.F.: Oh, yeah. My mother still plays church guitar. My mother's father was a great guitarist, home-wise (amateur). He used to play, and her brother used to play all the piano rags and I'd sit and watch him even before I was three years old. So I was around a lot of music.

R.D.R.: When did you decide you wanted to play?

V.F.: When I was around three; started on the saxophone when I was seven. I took the horn from my father's Victrola and bored holes in it and made a horn out of it. So he decided to buy me a horn after that. Seems like I've always been interested. I began on a C-melody sax; no I didn't, I began on a clarinet. But my first horn was a C-melody.

R.D.R.: C-melody, one thinks of the Trumbauer tradition.[1] Was there someone you were listening to?

V.F.: My father had some records just prior to Louis Armstrong, but they were more like comedy records. The saxophone player sounds like they're having fun, but I can't recall who they were.

R.D.R.: You say prior to Louis Armstrong...

V.F.: Yeah, because he (father) was crazy about Louis Armstrong. He got some records by Louis Armstrong around '27 or '28. I remember he had a couple of Al Jolson and Rudy Vallee's records, but the horn (comedy) players I can't remember who they were, but they weren't the ones that really interested me in the horn—it seems like that was, just happened to be my thing.

R.D.R.: Did you have anything to do with the Chicago New Music scene?

V.F.: No. I've been accused of teaching somebody something, but I don't know in what way that I did. Maybe they were listening to me. But I give out no instructions of any type. I maintain this music, you cannot teach it. I tell guys this every night 'cause they all want to study with me. I don't know what to tell them, no more than learn your chords and suffer. That's the way I learned it. They all want to know what type of mouthpiece, what type of reed. But this won't help, I've given guys my mouthpiece, it doesn't help them. It's a personal thing and in my opinion Jazz is a very personal thing—at least the way I play it, it is. First thing, you've got to be strong. I've been criticized very strongly through the years for this and that, but it never changed me, I just play the way I feel. I feel if they're going to survive, they've got to do this. Now if they're in this to get famous then I

[1]Frankie Trumbauer (1900-1956) played C-melody sax. Lester Young credited Trumbauer, a close associate of Bix Beiderbecke, as a prime influence on his own playing.

really can't tell them anything about it 'cause I never got famous. And if they want to make a lot of money I can't tell them about that either. Have to go to another guy that's done these things, maybe they can tell them. But if they just want to play music because they have to, which is the only reason I do it, I think you try to find a good instructor and teacher and learn the fundamentals; and from there it's like anything else. It's a creative thing. If you're in it for the plaudits you may be sort of disappointed. But if you're in it to express yourself, well... for me one of the greatest things is I'm able to play what I want to play and when I look back that's all I really want to do. It fulfills me to be able to sit down and think and be able to play that way. But it took me a lot of years to reach that and I did a lot of studying.

Another thing, by never having gotten famous, nothing was ever demanded of me, I could... Like my buddy Gene Ammons.[2] Gene and I went to school together, and he's been famous as long as I can remember. Now we were very close in some ways and whether or not Gene was happy or not I wouldn't try to say, but I know a lot of the time he'd play his solo. Now Gene Ammons is as creative as the next person, but you cut these hit records, and if you don't play those solos they say "but I still want to hear you solo." They wait for that solo. I've never had to do that, for no one knew any of my records anyway, so I was able to always just play 'cause they wouldn't bug me to try to copy what I have played. It really bugs me and I think bugs anyone who thinks he's creative to have to copy his records. Fortunately I haven't been in a position to have to do that.

R.D.R.: For you what is the most difficult thing about the Jazz life?

V.F.: The lack of money. Let's face it, no matter how creative you are, you still need money. And seemingly the more creative you are the less money you make. That's really sad, but I guess you have other things when you play creative, it's just unfortunate

[2]Gene Ammons (1925-1974), son of the great Boogie-Woogie pianist Albert Ammons, played tenor sax and was instrumental in developing the *big* modern Jazz tenor sound.

that you do have to pay bills. I think it would be better if this music was subsidized or something like that. The creative, this is something that you have to just live and grow with and as you get into it you get more and more creative.

R.D.R.: But if it were subsidized do you think it might lack an impetus?

V.F.: I thought about that too, it might take out some of the initiative. I don't really have the answers, I'm just stabbing in the dark. Like anything else, it's 360 degrees and I'm looking at it from my angle.

R.D.R.: Do you get invited to festivals and the like?

V.F.: No. Well, I've been very blessed the past couple of years I've been invited to a festival in Loren and another one in Belgium.

R.D.R.: But in the U.S.?

V.F.: No, I've never been invited.

R.D.R.: You worked for Sun Ra back when...

V.F.: Oh, yes, I was with Sun Ra sometime back in the '40s (1948/9), I can't remember just when. He's a person whatever you see, that's what he is.

R.D.R.: Did you do any recording with him?

V.F.: I never recorded with him—no, I think I did something but I don't know what, it's been so long ago. He was playing space music; we had a lot of space titles to his tunes.

R.D.R.: Did he live in a communal situation at that time?

V.F.: No, he just had a room or two at that time. But he's always thought that way, I think. He's like a godfather; he had that tendency to, ah, "come all ye children."

R.D.R.: There are conflicting reports about the Savoy "Bird At Home"[3] recording. It is now being claimed you're on that date.

[3]A private non-professional recording of Charlie Parker, in concert, later released on Savoy Records.

V.F.: Well I don't really know. I've heard that particular record and it sounds like me, but at that time, you know. . . . It sounds Pres-ish and of course I still play like Pres right to this day—well, he and Hawk.

R.D.R.: Your main inspiration?

V.F.: Oh, yeah. But about that record, we were up there (at the Pershing Ballroom) every weekend from about '46 to '50. George, my brother, says it's me, but I can't tell. Somebody that's Pres influenced and that could have been any of us.

R.D.R.: That recording wasn't done in the '50s?

V.F.: No. See after the '40s they started booking Rock acts, like Jackie Wilson, Andrew Tibbs, and they really went into another bag.

R.D.R.: But you did work with Horace Henderson.

V.F.: Yeah, that was in '40. I was very young, I borrowed my father's tuxedo. That was prior to going into the service. I learnt more in that band in one day than I learned in all the years I had been in music because he had all the top pros with him. He knew how to rehearse a band and that's a lost art. I stayed with him till I went into the service, in fact his band broke up because he was taking his band into the Army. I tried so hard to get in with it and somehow I didn't make it. But I made the Navy band.

R.D.R.: How long were you with the Horace Henderson Band?

V.F.: Oh, about a year, maybe a little bit more. Of course, Fletcher got famous but Horace wrote very well and he had a whole lot of his brother's charts in the book. It was an education to play with that band.

Billy Harper

Tenorist Billy Harper was born in 1943 in Texas, and continues in the tradition of the Texas tenors. Mr. Harper's playing is marked by its clean, articulated statements and muscular delivery. Previous to forming his own group his most notable work had been as a member of the Gil Evans band, Art Blakey's Jazz Messengers, the Thad Jones-Mel Lewis Jazz Orchestra and the Max Roach Quartet. When this interview was conducted in December 1978, Mr. Harper was a member of the Roach Quartet which was then appearing in Montreal, Quebec.

Ironically, while Billy Harper has recorded almost a dozen LPs under his own name, his only American release was a self-produced effort, "Capra Black," on the Strata East label. As a result, even though his records have received universal critical acclaim, Mr. Harper remains largely unknown to the general, casual, Jazz listener. It is obvious both in speaking with Mr. Harper and reviewing his discography that he is a man not only battling for the concerns of his art, but also fighting the compromising temptations often demanded of an artist desiring to have his work produced by American record companies.

R.D.R.: You worked with Gil Evans...

B.H.: Oh, yeah, I worked with Gil for such a long time, he was the first person I worked with when I got to New York, after staying there for one year. I came to New York about '66 and started working with him about '67. He just called me for rehearsals. There's a lot to gain from working with someone like Gil Evans. But all I was interested in at the time was just a matter of being functionable in music. But from people like Gil Evans you can gain much more knowledge and sensitivity of music.

R.D.R.: Before you came to New York, you had been involved with Rhythm and Blues, a lot?

B.H.: Not really. I mean I played Rhythm and Blues, you can't miss that in Texas. I did a lot of it, of course, but I did a lot of modern improvisation also. It was simply a stepping stone in growing music.

R.D.R.: I didn't mean to knock R'n'B.

B.H.: Oh, no, no, no, I still like Rhythm and Blues, I'm not saying it that way either. It's a stepping stone since the music had to relate to the Blues to me. You have to understand the Blues if you're going to really feel what "Jazz" or Black creative music is about. I played Rhythm and Blues at 16 and I used to sing before then, so I went through the whole thing and graduated and went further and started improvising. Some of my friends stopped at that level of Rhythm and Blues.

R.D.R.: Was there a reason you chose tenor?

B.H.: I used to sing and I just happened to walk by a store when I was small and saw the tenor saxophone with all those notes and all that complexity, yeah. I said what is that? That is interesting? How would you start? And that's the way I started with the saxophone. I got a saxophone for Christmas.

R.D.R.: How old?

B.H.: Eleven.

R.D.R.: Lesson, or working out on it by yourself?

B.H.: I didn't start taking lessons, in that way I was more sort of self-taught. I started learning technical structured things later in school.

R.D.R.: Were you listening to saxophonists?

B.H.: Oh, I was only listening to what was on the radio.

R.D.R.: At that time ('54) that would have been a lot of R'n'B.

B.H.: That's true and that's what I heard. But one of the inspirations in my life that sort of directed my particular growth who was my uncle that said, "Listen to this," and that was the music I'm playing.

R.D.R.: That was Earl Harper?

B.H.: That's right. He was a musician at heart. He went to school with Kenny Dorham and they both played trumpet and he stopped playing. He would take me to his house and he would sing solos and I would play what he's singing.

R.D.R.: Was there one particular player you singled out and listened to?

B.H.: At that time I listened so much to Kenny Dorham. And whoever was playing with Kenny at the time.

R.D.R.: At that time, the New York hard Bop scene.

B.H.: That's right, so I heard a lot of Horace Silver and Max Roach, Sonny Rollins.

R.D.R.: So you're a Texas tenor influenced by the New York school.

B.H.: Just about. The funny thing about that Texas thing, there's definitely some type of osmosis that happens. But when I was there I was not aware of Illinois Jacquet from Texas, I heard him from New York, on a record from New York.

R.D.R.: Deciding to come to New York, was that a big decision?

B.H.: It was no big decision, that was really what had to be done, it was automatic. Like you said, I was exposed to the New York musicians. New York musicians in the sense they go to New York and add something to New York and they became known as New York musicians, just as I have.

R.D.R.: But because you are from Texas you will also always be a "Texas tenor."

B.H.: Maybe, maybe, I don't mind that, that's all right 'cause I'd like to sort of expand the elements of the Texas tenor.

R.D.R.: But you do have a big, robust sound.

B.H.: Yeah, now maybe that's something that comes through the osmosis thing. 'Cause most of the people I heard sounded big like that (laughter). So that's the way it sounds, I mean that's the way it's supposed to sound, you know.

R.D.R.: Actually I've jumped ahead because before you came to New York you went to North Texas State.

B.H.: Yeah.

R.D.R.: You had to be one of the few...

B.H.: Few! Ha! (laughter).

R.D.R.: Few of "them" (laughter).

B.H.: I was the only one (laughter) in the Number One Band, One O'Clock Lab Band. Of course there were more Blacks in the music department, maybe four or five in the "Jazz" department. Maybe two would be ready for the One O'Clock Band and I happen to make it.

R.D.R.: The emphasis was on technique, or the technical.

B.H.: Yeah, that's the big thing. But at that particular time, that was the '60s and they had to deal with the problem of trying to get the idea of having the band integrated over to the other people who were running the school after being made aware of this. It's such a funny thing now that I've gotten away from there,

Freddie Hubbard

Paul Quinichette with Count Basie
circa 1951

Milt Jackson

Cecil Taylor

© David D. Spitzer

Sun Ra

© David D. Spitzer

Milt Hinton

© Susan M. Rusch

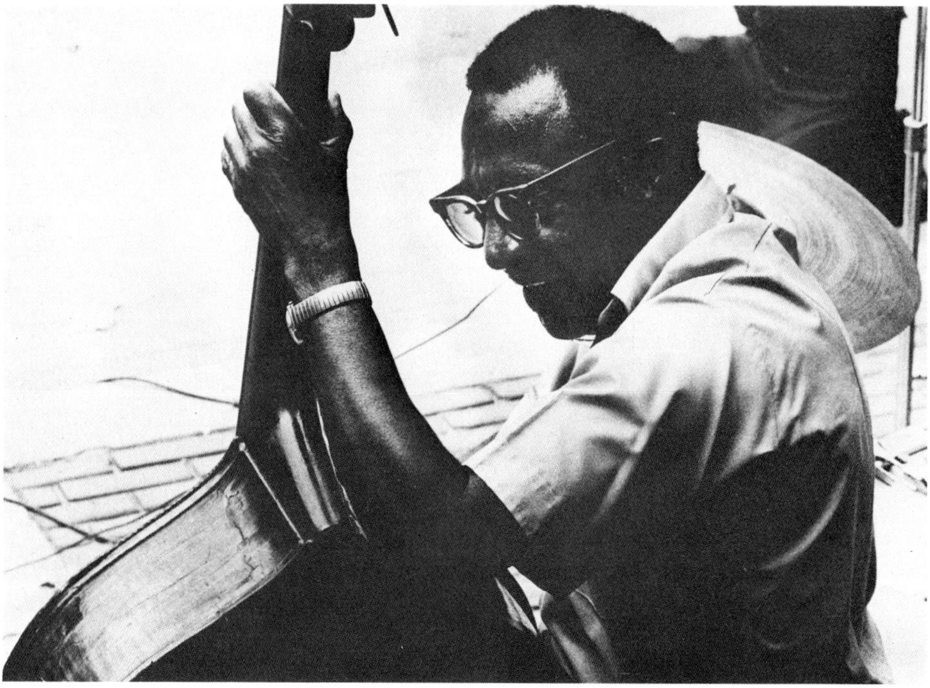

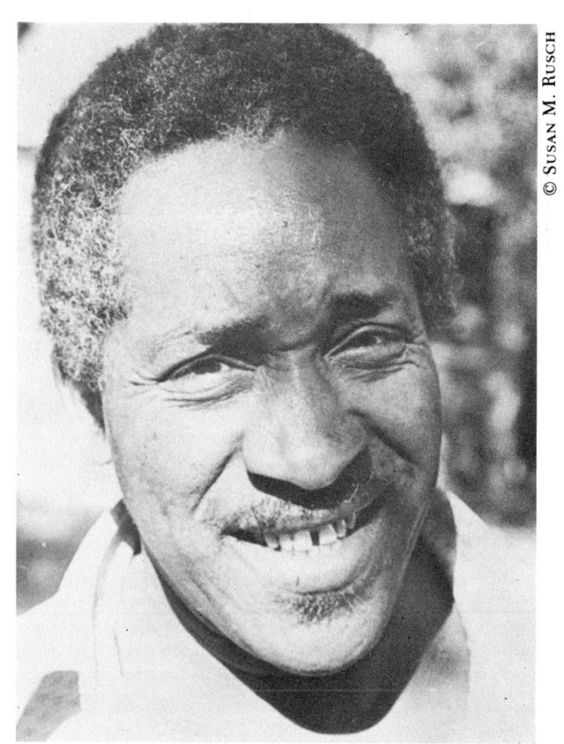

Von Freeman

Billy Harper

Art Blakey

Bill Dixon

they're playing music from Black culture and I'm striving to get in it—that's ridiculous (laughter).

They had their standards strongly emphasizing the technical and that's an easy way to weed out a lot of people, so I just worked hard and didn't worry about it, they were going through the problem because I was ready even as a sophomore. There was some stage that I decided I have to just put everything into it and work hard as I can. It doesn't matter about the band, it's that I have to get to this particular level that's in my head, because I'm going to New York (laughter). One semester I stopped all the other courses and just practiced every day.

R.D.R.: You listen to the One O'Clock Bands and they are in some ways very impressive, but very few, I don't even think a handful, seem to go on and make names for themselves in creative improvised music.

B.H.: Yeah, well, that's another thing I had to discover. When I was there I was not trying to get to finally be accepted in this band. I was trying to do as much as I could do and had to do for me.

R.D.R.: When you finally did come to New York did you naively feel this enrollment/degree were credentials for you—an "in" to the Jazz world?

B.H.: No. I stayed (at North Texas State University). I was going to leave and come to New York when I was 19. My uncle and parents said, "Look, you have to finish school, it's important to have this degree," and it hasn't helped me since (laughter). But for Blacks, of course I understand what he meant. I knew the degree and all of that had nothing to do with how much I could play.

The basic thing that I got from the school was discipline, and that's what you get from any school if you really apply yourself. Discipline, that's all and learning how to write and orchestrate for big bands.

R.D.R.: Aside from your uncle was there a strong tradition of music in your family?

B.H.: Oh sure, I was raised by grandparents. Grandfather was the minister (African Methodist Episcopal Church). My grandmother was in church every Sunday and I learned much about the source from that church. My family was into arts and a lot of things, so I sang, acted and did art at one time.

R.D.R.: Reviewing your own recordings from "Capra Black" ('73) to the Japanese Denon efforts ('78), your music seems to go from a restless agitation to a more pensive quality. Does that parallel you over those years?

B.H.: No, I think it sort of relates to what I feel in my character. "Capra Black" meant Black Capricorn, and as a Capricorn the mood is related to what you were describing—the restless kind of thing involved the energy that involved the sign. But there's also a solid character involved.

R.D.R.: Well, there is on "Cry Of Hunger" (from "Capra Black"). In fact, that has such a lilting, melancholy, happy feel to it, so incongruous with the title.

B.H.: A lot of the compositions I write and name are done so because of an inner meaning. An example, one of the later tunes I've written will be called "Knowledge of Self." The tune, when I play it doesn't sound like that's the title it should have, because it sounds happy. It sounds playful in a way and I don't play playful tunes, at least I don't see them as playful (laughter). But inside that feeling of dance in a kind of way to me it means that the soul dances. Because of this knowledge of self the soul dances.

"Cry of Hunger," the turmoil and agitation in the beginning expressed the kind of thing Blacks are involved in all over the world, the strife, the struggle—that's mainly what it portrays. But underneath the struggle every one of us, whether we are aware of it or not, have to have something inside that is stable and strong, and so that expresses perhaps the happy and the smooth side you hear.

R.D.R.: Your playing is very strong, you don't seem ever to waste notes or play frivolously. Where do you see it going?

B.H.: I know exactly what you mean because I approach music that way. I don't really like to play anything frivolous, and that's why I was mentioning that tune to you, 'cause to me it's a little more playful than anything I would usually write. I believe in a no-nonsense approach to playing because there's a lot that has to be done in music, very much has to be done. And very much can be done even before going out to what most people call "free."[1] It's easy, very easy for me to play that, and that's a part of it too. That's an expression of part of the whole too. Very often I feel that I'm taking a new direction and I've found something new. To other people they may not hear it, but I know exactly what it is and I know exactly where I am on the steps on the ladder that I am at that particular point. What is new and how I can use it to further the direction.

R.D.R.: And growth.

B.H.: I feel I will always grow.

R.D.R.: But I mean not just in accumulating a depth of knowledge but expanding the perspectives of it...

B.H.: The evolution, yes of course, that's exactly the way I mean, that's how I want to live. I've decided life is growth and learning and I don't mean just an accumulation of knowledge. I am responsible for my growing so it's about evolving, not just gaining knowledge, but I have to discover more so the music has to grow, that's the only way I'll be playing.

R.D.R.: You seem to have an affinity for drummers—you've been primarily affiliated with Max Roach, Elvin Jones, Art Blakey and even Mel Lewis-Thad Jones' Band.

B.H.: Yeah, that's right. That's one of the key things to my music, I've always been attracted to drums and I play drums a little.

[1] "Free Jazz" evolved out of music developed in the '60s though the music of artists like Charlie Mingus, Eric Dolphy, Cecil Taylor, Ornette Coleman, and John Coltrane; improvised music with disciplining structures but free of many of the restrictive laws of harmony, melody, tone and form associated with earlier Jazz styles.

When I used to practice so much in school I'd get tired and go play drums.

R.D.R.: I play drums and when I get tired I go blow the sax. So there! (Laughter)

B.H.: I don't mean it's easy (laughter). I write a lot of music from drums, I feel so much rhythm. That's why I say there's so many things that can be done. I feel so much rhythm, that's why so many of the tunes I write are rhythmy, 'cause sometimes they are written from the drums. Sometimes the rhythmic concept is there and I base everything on that. That's how "Capra Black" came about.

R.D.R.: Did you seek the drummers out?

B.H.: No, it just happened. With Blakey I always wanted to play with Blakey, so I found him in that instance. Max I think found me; Elvin and I sort of got together.

So the drummers and I have always had natural rapport 'cause I feel what they're doing.

R.D.R.: You made a recording with Charles Earland...

B.H.: That happened when I was working with Lee Morgan. Charles got to me through Lee who was on the date also, so he asked if I would make it and I said "yeah." I never thought about it. I went into the studio and we recorded and I never got a chance to think about it much, except while I was playing.

R.D.R.: Are you satisfied with most of your recordings?

B.H.: Yeah, because to me part of what I'm supposed to be doing as a musician and growing is to make myself the tool for creating this truth, and as long as I feel that way at the time that I'm playing, it's fine. As long as I feel I've been truthful to what I'm supposed to do right, then it's okay.

R.D.R.: Talking and watching you I'd think you'd find it hard to be part of a big band.

B.H.: That is true. With Gil (Evans) that band had much more freedom than Thad Jones, which is coming from a very traditional point of view and I felt a little cramped in that situation... not enough space for me because I like to really stretch out. I could stretch out more with Gil Evans. But there was quite a bit to gain from being around such greatly written music as the Thad Jones Orchestra. So I learned other things... how to... ah... how to ah... to ah... you know, wait.... (laughter)

R.D.R.: Before that you had been with Art Blakey, why did you leave?

B.H.: Well, it was a matter of money, I just felt it was time to get more money, but parted on very good terms and I really respect him and he's a dynamo. And he has a good band today too.

R.D.R.: You consider yourself a Messenger?

B.H.: In a way, yes. I don't know if I would consider myself limited to being a Jazz Messenger, but I certainly consider myself a messenger; and coming through the Jazz Messengers has something to do with that too.

R.D.R.: Tell us about the first time you met Elvin Jones.

B.H.: He was playing at Slugs[2] and I had a hard time dealing with him then. I went five nights straight asking about playing, and nothing; on the last night he finally let go and said, "Okay." When I came up he jumped off and put Philly Jones on the drums (laughter). This was '67 or '66.

R.D.R.: Slugs was a tough place.

B.H.: Too tough. But they are typical of the joints musicians have had to play in. It's unfortunate the music has to come through the back door as an illegitimate child.

R.D.R.: Have you been impressed by any of the Euro-Jazz?

B.H.: Impressed in positive and negative ways. To me it seems they are very concerned with control of images to eventually say *this* is *the* Jazz. I've heard musicians who may not be able to

[2]Slugs was a New York City nightclub which catered to New Music in the tough frontier environment of the Lower East Side.

swing, play free because it's a good escape for them—so I've been impressed by this negatively. They haven't gone back to the roots of the music to understand it's simply academic and intellectual only. I mean that's a part of it.

R.D.R.: But talking about that root some of the Europeans are beginning to incorporate their own unique roots into creative improvised music. Some of the Afro-English players in England and some of the German and other western European artists are doing this also.

B.H.: I have heard other musicians in Europe who do have a feeling for the real thing, but I don't know if they understand about developing it.

R.D.R.: But some of it is not necessarily about a traditional root Jazz experience but utilizes a creative improvisation which has traditionally been Jazz.

B.H.: In that way it's okay if it's understood as coming from there. To me the essence of the music has to be related to the swing feeling that's innate in "Jazz" music. I don't mean it can't be free but some kind of way it has to be connected to the real essence of the music, it's not just about sitting up and playing some notes and then improvising some sounds on those notes. It's not like that, but some people have that concept in Europe, I understand.

R.D.R.: How do you assess what you have done?

B.H.: The main thing I have done is to try and be very truthful to this gift that I have. I recognize the gift and I know that I have to be very truthful to it. I've tried to follow the path in this particular truth. What happens on the outside, how much exposure, how much everybody knows about me or something is secondary. The main thing is about being truthful. I could have recorded a long time ago with a company that would have had me doing some fusion, many companies.

I have realized myself as the instrument from the source that the music comes, I'm just the tool.

R.D.R.: Do you see greatness?

B.H.: Greatness is flowing through, its not me, but it's flowing. I see god as greatness.

R.D.R.: Anything else you'd like to say?

B.H.: Sometimes people are programmed to listen to things that the media says to listen to. Which means that they're not giving enough of themselves to really hear it themselves or let it touch them. Most people grow up and then learn to close themselves out to feeling, to loving, to being. When they do that it's difficult to really listen to the music, and so basically they're going on programming. So they read that Jazz is dead, Jazz is alive or something like that, and Jazz has always been alive.

R.D.R.: More truthfully it's been the public or potential reviewers that are alive or dead.

B.H.: That's right. Everybody just has to watch out for programming.

R.D.R.: How long before you see yourself as pretty much exclusively leading your own group?

B.H.: Shouldn't be very long. The thing that's difficult about that, because people have not heard so much about me in the States, it's hard to get booked in clubs. It's easier for me to play in Europe. But I'm going to do as much as I can do without prostituting anything, without changing any of my values.

Art Blakey

Drummer Art Blakey is one of the great institutions of Jazz. Born in Pittsburgh in 1919, he rose up through the Swing era and was a member, from 1944-47, of the ground breaking big band of Billy Eckstine. The Eckstine band employed at one time or another many of the best of the then emerging New Wave (Bop) players of the post-Swing period. After freelancing in the early '50s, Mr. Blakey began leading a group called the Jazz Messengers. It was through the Jazz Messengers that Art Blakey refined a distinctive influential drum style and helped establish a whole school of Bop known as Hard Bop. In addition, the Messengers have taken on the character of a school with Blakey its director, and with many of the Bop masters from the '50s into the '80s its graduates. Included in the list of alumni are Clifford Brown, Horace Silver, Hank Mobley, Kenny Dorham, Jackie McLean, John Coltrane, Lee Morgan, Johnny Griffin, Bobby Timmons, Chuck Mangione, Freddie Hubbard, Keith Jarrett, Don Byrd, Wynton Marsalis, Wayne Shorter, Billy Harper, Curtis Fuller, Woody Shaw, Cedar Walton, just to name a few.

I interviewed Mr. Blakey in November 1980 in Montreal, Quebec.

R.D.R.: Do you ever get tired of playing "Tunisia"?[1]

A.B.: Yeah, you get tired of playing things like that, tired of playing "Blues March" and playin' "Moanin'," but that's your bread and butter music, that's what it is. To keep from getting tired of it, is to have different cats come in, play different versions of it. There're other kids that come along that need a break, put the (old) guys out there on their own. Get some new talent, have to have something to look forward to. It keeps the group live and fresh, it keeps it from getting stale. It's all right to play the same things over if it's different versions, different approaches—you need that thing to keep it alive. You go every night and you hear something different, I think it's the most wonderful music there is, that I have run into, in my life. I think it came about as a fluke, somebody goofed. It's really freedom, it's spiritual, you see democracy in its truest form, socialism in its truest form—there's everything there. And it's the highest level of performance on a musical instrument. Nobody can surpass a Jazz musician on a musical instrument, nobody. And the quality of musicians I see today, deportment, they are 150% better musicians than before.

R.D.R.: I think many are a little cold.

A.B.: Well, I'm only talking about their deportment, the way they act, the way they present themselves. Years before it was the pressure of the society that made the musicians act like they did. I'm glad it isn't like that no more, these kids have a better opportunity. And they got guys around, Max Roach, Monk, I'm still here, they got people to show them good things. I think in the not too distant future we're goin' to see more of the Art Tatum, more Charlie Parker. They don't come around all the time, maybe 50 years or so, but it's coming 'round that time. But I'll tell you what, you'll never see it coming, it always comes from out of the left field. When I first saw Charlie Parker I said, "Oh, my god." The man was hoboing, got off the train in Chicago and

[1] "Night In Tunisia," written by Dizzy Gillespie and originally titled "Strange Interlude," is one of the Bop anthems and an often played standard in the Messengers' repertoire, as are other tunes like "Blues March" and "Moanin'."

went over to hear Earl Hines. Walked into the dressing room, said, "Can I look at your horn"—looked at the horn, hadn't even cleaned himself up yet—just played. Saxophone player, named "Goon," played with Earl Hines, said, "What," went and got him a clean shirt, gave him a horn and pushed him out on that stage.

When I saw Clifford Brown, I said, "Well, Jesus, I need a trumpet player," so Charlie Parker said, "When you get to Philadelphia and play in the Blue Note on Ridge Avenue your trumpet player will be there." I said, "Who was it?" He said, "Don't worry about that, you just... uh... and he will be." And we get there and in the dressing room somebody's back there blowing. This guy had a stocking cap on, suspenders and blowing his horn, warming up. He sounds beautiful. So Ike Quebec was with me at the time, he said, "Man, why don't you tell me you're getting a farmer to play trumpet." (Laughter) I say, "Well, I don't know, Bird tells me..." He said, "Man, Jesus Christ man, plus he ain't nothin' but a kid." And he (Clifford Brown) had a very high voice and was very sweet. So I said, "Well come on, we're going to hit." He (Brown) came out and played the first chorus of it and after he played the first chorus Ike turned around and cussed me out, "Dirty so and so, how come you didn't tell me the kid could play like that?" (Laughter) That's what happened, he upset everybody. You don't know where they're coming from.

R.D.R.: Man, could he dance on that trumpet!

A.B.: Aw man—fantastic! And just as sweet and a hell of a concert pianist.

R.D.R.: I've always felt the Birdland dates[2] with Horace, Brownie, Lou Donaldson and Curley Russell are some of the finest live moments in Jazz.

A.B.: It was just one of those times and it was the right combination, it was a good spirit and the guys really loved each other. The group has to be just the right combination, like they

[2]Recorded live at Birdland 2/21/54 and issued on Blue Note Records 81522 and 81521.

say, one rotten apple will spoil the whole barrel if he's wrong. And you being a leader, have to be very careful, you're the last one to find out what's happening in your own group. It isn't always the music, it's how the group gets along spiritually, how they like each other. Some guys get together right away and can mark it.

R.D.R.: One group that never seemed to jell was the unit with (Chuck) Mangione and (Keith) Jarrett It never seemed to get the Messenger ah...

A.B.: Spirit.

R.D.R.: Right.

A .B.: Well, that was a fact. It was really a misfit. The reason why things were so terribly unbalanced there was because we had Keith, who was a very accomplished musician. And there were other musicians in the band who were growing. Sometimes a man has so much talent he would get bored waiting for the rest of the cats to catch up. And Keith could play other instruments too and he knew what the saxophone player was doing wrong, what the trumpet player was doing wrong. He was in the band because of me, because he liked me. But it's like a kid in school, put him in the wrong class and he gets bored. The group that we got now (Robert Watson, James Williams, Charles Fambrough, Wynton Marsalis, James Emery, Billy Pierce) I think is one of the best, not *the* best, groups I ever had. The minute you hear it you'll recognize it.

R.D.R.: Idrees Sulieman, in a *Cadence* interview (Sept. '79), said that when you were with Fletcher Henderson you were "a terrible drummer" and credits Dizzy Gillespie with "teaching" you to play drums during the Eckstine period. True?

A.B.: Oh, Idrees' crazy. That's the only reason I had the job, the only reason I had the job. I don't think he heard me that much. What I was playing was kind of different from the drummer that his band was using, maybe he just couldn't understand it. I just know that's not true.

And when Idrees got to Boston I had a 14-piece band and I was induced to leave Fletcher Henderson in Boston to form a band at the Tick Tock Club. I didn't even know him that well and when I did meet him in New York he was into something else, politics and religion, all that stuff. I thought it was very personal, religion is your business, I just want to play music. The reason I was with Fletcher Henderson, Duke Ellington, Lucky Millender, those guys, was because I was a guy who could keep time and play what they wanted me to play. I never went with a band to play Art Blakey. I knew better than that. I played what they wanted. I had been a kid sitting around listening to their arrangements, so when the time came, something happened to their drummer—dropped—drop out, you know. Like Jo Jones, with Basie, he would come and get me. Sonny Greer with Duke, if they were around somewhere near Pittsburgh they would send for me. In those days, the young kids got the opportunity to play in the big bands, sit next to the high experienced musicians and that way learn a lot. That's where I learned a lot about how to play. How to play drums and things.

But when I was in Boston, Billy (Eckstine) sent for me and I took my trombone player (Marion Hazel) and trumpeter (Walter Harris) and he hired both of them. Billy heard about me from musicians in the band. Anyway, it wasn't a question of time, maybe they didn't understand what I was playing, I didn't understand my damn self what I was playing. I was just trying to do something and trying to do something different. One thing you had to do that Chick Webb taught me, was that you had to identify yourself. If you don't have a melody instrument you had to identify yourself. Chick Webb brought the drums from the background to the front—it was no longer 14 musicians and the drummer. It was 15 musicians. I began to listen to him because he made more sense to me. Other drummers I began to listen to for time was Ray Bauduc and for finesse and technique Sid Catlett. The time I came along, Idrees was probably listening to Western drums from Kansas City, like Jo Jones plays the high-hat sock cymbal, where Eastern drums you play on the top cymbal. First drummer I saw do that and play with his bass drum and didn't have no sock cymbal was Kenny Clarke, with the Mills Blue Rhythm Orchestra. And that was Kenny Clarke in the late '20s or early '30s. And Joe Watts taught him to play drums, read music, and Kenny Clarke is a vibraphone player—and can play 'em. And this is where I developed, from these kind of people. I knew I was right, but it was a little different; but I was always the kind of kid who could come in and play and keep the time. So I don't know where he (Idrees Sulieman) got that idea. . . well he was young and that's the way he thought at the time. He was a little confused. It was a little different what I was doing—they put down when things begin to change.

R.D.R.: The three things that immediately identify you is your high-hat chomp-chomp-chomp, your rim or stick shots and of course that press roll.

A.B.: The way I try to identify myself is just making the press roll. I got a friend out in California, he's got a great big automobile spring hanging in his window. He says it's Art Blakey's sock cymbal spring (laughter). I never paid no attention to that, I just say that's the way it's suppose to be, just keep time, get swinging. And the roll. Sid Catlett told me that, he said, "Son, when you're in trouble, roll." He was something else. Drummers all got something to say. The music down the years, the drummers have really got it together. Now electronics are here to stay and you got to learn how to deal with them.

R.D.R.: I couldn't see it in the Messengers.

A.B.: The reason why I haven't is because electronics really takes away from the human element.

R.D.R.: Could you really visualize, say, an electric piano in your group?

A.B.: Yeah, if it sounds like a piano (laughter).

R.D.R.: Let me go back again to this interview. Mr. Sulieman says, "We founded the Messengers (in the '40s), in fact it broke up because there was a vote in the band whether I could be the leader or Art Blakey. But Art says, Well, if I'm not the leader I'm not going to play."

A.B.: That's not right at all. The band had 17 members and Idrees, if he were a leader, would have a band now. He never was a leader; he's a great musician, but that does not make him a great leader. It's a whole different thing.

We had the 17 Messengers and most of the guys were Muslims, this was between '47 and '50. Guys started rehearsing, and the guy doing most of the writing was Kenny Dorham. But at that time, big bands were going out, not coming in. It was a financial disaster. I was leading the band, and I couldn't carry no weight like that. I had four children and no wife and I couldn't be bothered with that—so the band broke up. So Horace Silver got Hank Mobley and Kenny Dorham and Doug Watkins and myself and said, "Art, you should be the leader since you have more experience than the rest of the guys and we'd like to have you up here with us." And I said, "Well, what should we call the band?" He said, "We can't call it 17 Messengers, so we'll call it Art Blakey and the Jazz Messengers." And that's the way the band started and this is what Horace named it and it's stuck ever since. We didn't put the band to go worldwide and make a lot of money, we were just trying to make some gigs and play, because we're tired of goin' on gigs and jamming, with a pick-up band, play the same old tunes. People got tired of that shit and I could see they were getting tired and I don't like chaos anyhow. I like freedom, but without discipline is chaos. So we wrote arrangements, got sharp—got some suits, started payin' attention to the audience and put it together. It first started out being a cooperative thing, but it didn't work because it wasn't equal. I had the weight and it had to go my way and Horace went on his own and that's when we began to bring different cats in, I just kept goin' with it. Well, somebody got to stay here and keep the store and it's been continuing ever since.

R.D.R.: How did John Gilmore join the band?

A.B.: Well, he was with Sun Ra and he came from Chicago and I made some recordings with him on Blue Note. I liked the way he played, very hip. So it came we needed a tenor player, we were on our way to Japan, and Lee Morgan went and got John Gilmore and he played very well. He made the tour with us, but he had commitments.

R.D.R.: He says you fired him.

A.B.: No, I didn't fire John, I would never fire John. I ain't never fired nobody. I get angry, but I give them enough rope to hang themselves. Now I've had groups together where all the rest of the cats have gotten together and sanctioned against another musician, and I had to let him go—but it wasn't on my decision alone. I never fired John Gilmore, I criticized him because he'd be talking the way he was thinking. The way he thought about life and what he believed in and why he would put down other people. I didn't think it was right. He was young and running off the top of his head, don't tell me that Lester Young steals from him, or Coltrane steals things from him—that's not true. He's off. One thing leads to another, give everybody credit for what they have done. But I loved his playing and he's learned how to be a terrific drummer, too. I wasn't concerned about anything but his playing. He'd be telling me about his fans on Mars or Jupiter, but I said it's the fans on this planet we're concerned with, not back there.

R.D.R.: How did you get to playing piano?

A.B.: Survival. I had to eat. I just know I didn't want to work. I stopped in 7th grade, got kicked out. I was workin' steel mills and coal mines, I was a kid and they had child labor. I couldn't make that thing, I'd work my brains out. I'd get tired, rest on my shovel, boss come around... "What you doin'—bla bla bla, so and so, you're fired son." I just told him "Listen Big Red, you little ass so and so..." Anyway I was playin' in two or three keys, shit, I went out there and got me a gig. All I wanted to do was survive. I made so much money in the tip box, I was the biggest money maker in my house.

R.D.R.: What kind of musical routine?

A.B.: I used to make up dirty songs in E-flat. We'd have a little spinet piano and I'd move to different tables. Just filth and they loved it and I'd get 10, 20, 40 dollars tips a night. And I met a guy named Hitchcock, a trombone player could really play and we had a gig in a bar, trombone and piano all in B-flat, E-flat, A-flat, I couldn't get out of them. And then I had this 14-piece band and we made $15 a week. Cats dressed in tails and played in the club. They brought in Tondalayo and Lopez, an act from New York Raymond Scott had. I didn't know nothin' about music and I pretended. I'll never forget that ego, a lesson for my life. I'd tell the brass (with authority), "All right brass run it down!" And the brass would run it down and pow, we'd get to the piano part and I'd sit there, couldn't read. I say (to the band) that didn't sound too good, why don't you do it again (laughter). Tondalayo sitting there waiting and waiting and she played the record again. I had on a big terry cloth shirt and a towel around my neck, sittin' out front of the band, chair turned backward, and I went over to the piano again, and they ran it down again and it came to the piano part and the band comes pow! I looked at them and said, "All you son of a bitches know god damned well I can't read!" (laughter). So this guy sitting in the corner said, "Let me try it." And so he ran down through it like a dose of Epsom salts and that was Erroll Garner. And that was the end of my piano career.

R.D.R.: You moved right over to drums?

A.B.: Yes, sir, course I was always running up showing the drummer, Skippy, how to play the drums, I didn't have them, but I always liked them. But Erroll played, and played so well the cat who owned the place was sitting over in the corner, he called me over, says, "Hey, Art I think the kid should play the piano and you should play the drums." I said, "Listen man, this is my band, you can't tell me how to run it." He said, "Now how long you been here? You want to stay don't you?" He had a 350 magnum on his side. I said, "Hell, yes, I want to stay." He said, "Well, you dumb bastard, get up there and play the drums." I've been playing drums ever since. Just a matter of survival.

R.D.R.: Was your family musical?

A.B.: All the Blakey's were musicians except my father and my father hated musicians. But I didn't know my father was my father till I was 15 and I got ready to get married. I had two chicks knocked up and I had to get married right away or you go to jail in them times. So he had to sign for me, that's when I found out he was my father and I'd see him almost everyday but I didn't know he was my dad. I was raised by another family. The Blakey's were in another groove, they were mulattoes and at that time they couldn't have nothing to do with Black. And my mother died when I was about 6 months. I was raised by my mother's first cousin. I went to school in Pittsburg under the name Art Parran, people know me as Art Parran. She brought me home from my mother's funeral and that was the first time my father saw her since they got married and he denied me. So (Mrs. Parran) took me home and her husband says, "You bring that Black son-of-a-bitch in here, I'm goin'." So she says, "Just a minute." She went upstairs and packed all his clothes and put them on the front porch, said, "You goin', goodbye." And that was the end of it. And she was the one who was responsible for me, she always tell me I was her child, 'cause she loved me. Then I heard rumors and people tell me, "Ya you know . . . " and I got really embarrassed about it and that's what really made me go to work. 'Cause I felt very bad, this woman be struggling, trying to help, working for $.50 a day and car fare and I couldn't deal with it. I couldn't think in school, with the stuff they was teaching us—I couldn't go for it. And the only opportunity open to me at that time wasn't even fighting, it was music, so I went into music to survive. I wasn't about to do labor, I couldn't do it. I always wanted to be a lawyer, I think I could have been a hell of a lawyer. I taught myself to read and the little mathematics I know.

R.D.R.: With all due respect, we don't need more lawyers, we need more Art Blakeys.

A.B.: This was my contribution, to get with music. I was forced really. I didn't have a choice. Now I feel so bad about the young people today. They got so many choices they get put down because it's hard for them to make a decision. I don't know what I would do. But leave them alone or encourage them, they'll find their way, don't put them down. I'm glad I was born (Oct. 11, 1919) in the time I was born. I think I had a wonderful time and I had a ball, honest to god I had a ball. And today things overall are 100% better than they were and it's going to get better.

R.D.R.: And your health is good?

A.B.: They say number one. My father died when he was 103.

R.D.R.: It's amazing the shape you're in with all the abuse.

A.B.: It wasn't nothin' to being in drugs when I started using drugs, you pass by the drugstore and they had cocaine in the window on a machine. Just go in a drugstore and buy some cocaine. Wasn't nothin' wrong with that until it got into neighborhoods with children and then to the middle class and then rich people, then oh, oh. It's been around since biblical days, but it got out of hand. I wanted to know just what it was all about.

R.D.R.: You stopped by yourself?

A.B.: Yup, but I paid for it—but I never missed a job. Music kept me together. If I could make it to the bandstand I was all right. I started stopping about 1963. It's a difficult thing getting to use drugs and not let them use you. But everybody got self-righteous about it instead of coming right down, up front about it. *This is this and that is that* and I know I'm right because I told my kids about it and not a one of them use narcotics, not a one! And I sired seven of them and we are tight.

R.D.R.: What do you think about drum battles?

A.B.: Well, it's a lot of fun to play with drums. But you're putting the people on because drums are a visual thing and you do what people like to see, not really getting it together.

R.D.R.: Do you listen to other drummers?

A.B.: No, and I'll tell you why. Everytime I listen to drummers, I don't care who it is, it could be you, if I came in a couple of nights, three or four times and listened, I'm gonna steal something you've got.

R.D.R.: I'm not worried (laughter).

A.B.: You'd be surprised, you can learn something from everybody. And those little things you do I can turn it around to this. My ears are so big it just stays in my head and it takes away from my creativity. I just start stealing (laughter).

R.D.R.: You often use a marching motif, do you trace that back to anyone?

A.B.: Well, a lot of people like that, they like the music. It swings, I like that beat. A lot of cats call it shuffle beat, it's not.

R.D.R.: How were things when you first got to New York?

A.B.: I wasn't playing in New York, I was just around observing. I didn't want to, but Monk is the guy, say, "Hey, man, come on, come on." And we would go to jam sessions and he would have Bud Powell and me with him. And, "Oh, oh, here come Monk with those cats." They don't want to let Bud play and they don't want to let me play. So we just get 'em all off the stage and me and Bud would play. Then Monk would come up and play. Then all the guys would rush back up on the stand and want to play with Monk—"Naw, let's go," and we'd (all) walk out. But this happened like all over New York, this is the kind of guy Thelonious was. What made the musicians do that, the gigs were so few everybody had formed cliques. And they felt every time you walked in, all the musicians, they felt threatened. And the only place you could go and play was Minton's.[3] "Lockjaw" (Eddie Davis) had the band there. He didn't give a damn who came in, he just let everybody play—he was a ball, man. And when Lockjaw would go out and do other things he had it fixed so Thelonious Monk come in and I came with him and Al McKibbon. And we started making records and different things.

R.D.R.: Do you think Monk will play again?

[3]A Harlem nightclub whose open afterhours jamming ambiance helped incubate early Bop concepts developed in the mid '40s.

A.B.: . . . . I hope so. I think he'll play if he lives, he's got to play or he'll die, that's the kind of musician he is.[4]

R.D.R.: How about Miles Davis?

A.B.: I don't know, he's up and around. I think the whole thing is, now's the time for him to decide what he's gonna do, put his ego away. He's bald-headed now. I think he should go get himself some acupuncture, or go get him a rug or cut it all off, he's still gorgeous.[5]

R.D.R.: Perhaps he should buy a used one from Earl Hines.

A.B.: Yeah, I died when I saw that. I said, "Hey, Gate, where'd you get that chinchilla cap?" (laughter). He didn't pay any attention to me. I love him, he is something else. I learned so much from him about band leading. He's a dealer. Earl Hines had me so tight when I was in his combo. He bought us all bathrobes and pajamas and he'd send in flowers every morning to put in your bathrobe lapel—"You never know when the press is coming." (laughter). The curtain never comes down, Gate (laughter). He's nice. I played with him in the '50s.

R.D.R.: That late?

A.B.: Yeah. He went out with a combo; he had Etta Jones, Harold Clark, Bennie Green, Jonah Jones and myself and I think Tommy Potter. Osie Johnson came in and took my place. Oh, Gate was so mad, he wanted to beat me up. We had a good thing going, but I had to get out of there, it wasn't my thing. I wanted to get myself together so I went and joined Buddy DeFranco.

R.D.R.: That was a strange combination. I don't think you complemented each other.

A.B.: Well, he had a hell of a rhythm section. He had Curley Russell and Gene Wright and Kenny Drew and myself. We had a ball back there, we didn't care what he did, just set fire to it. But

[4]Thelonious Monk died Feb. 17, 1982. His last public appearance was in the mid '70s.

[5]Miles Davis returned to active playing and recording in the early '80s.

he was a fine person, something else. He turned down a lot of opportunities because of us. Everything wasn't roses back then. They'd expect Buddy DeFranco to come in with an all White band. He'd show up with us and some places we'd come in the Midwest, Idaho, we get our reservations and come in to check in and we say, "What you mean there's no room, we have reservations." They'd say, "Naw, we got a football game today, your rooms are all gone." Buddy would say, "What! Football in August?" (laughter). He'd come in and raise hell; he's a hell of a man.

R.D.R.: Well, you got your head cracked open in the South didn't you?

A.B.: Oh, sure, but that was through my ignorance also, but, I didn't know enough. I was down in the (late) '30s with Fletcher Henderson. It was something down there at that time. The people don't know, they think it was the (Freedom) bus ride; shit, it was the musicians who broke down all that stuff. We'd go down to the South and the first place you go was across the tracks to the police station to find out where you could live—there wasn't no Black hotels or anything. Then you go with the police and wake up some women in a rooming house, or the undertaker— "Hey, Sally, get up, we got some coons out here want cha." That kind of stuff. And that continues right through till the Billy Eckstine band. The Eckstine band got together, it was very frightening—it was a young band and they weren't going for nothin'. Everybody in the band was armed. Fats Navarro was a hell of a marksman; he'd go hunting with a .45 and get rabbits. We were traveling down there and we had to play army camps everyday and we had a bus during war-time, burning diesel fuel, you know how that went down in the South. What the police would say about that, a big bus full of coons and a White driver and he was a Southerner too. I can see the changes. The war brought about changes because we had Fletcher's band we had to integrate, it didn't make no difference then, just so you could play. And Fletcher would play for the Elks whatever down there and they had a big screen in front of the band and all White musicians had to blacken their faces. And then they see us on the bus (laughter), "Hey, one of those boys look like a White boy—what was your daddy, boy?" Then with Eckstine, during the war on trains where all the Blacks had to ride right behind the engine and all the smoke and you're in there with all the soldiers, babies and women and you got drums, bass fiddle. But, that band was really frightening 'cause I knew they weren't going to take nothing. I saw them rip a club apart in Boston when some people came in from the South and made some cracks and the management didn't take care of business. They ripped the club apart and this was Boston, Massachusetts.

I got ran out of Greenville, Mississippi, by the sheriff when I was with Fletcher. I was going with a beautiful Black girl, but I didn't know it was the sheriff's woman. And she was Black and beautiful, woohoo! Blacker than I ever dreamed of being, so Black she was just purple, just velvet, just beautiful. So you never know what was going on, especially in the state of Mississippi, Georgia, and Alabama.

R.D.R.: Yeah, people disappeared down there.

A.B.: Oh, boy, yes sir, they found that out too. But if you're smart you can get by them, but if you go try to be a wise guy . . . I'm not interested in trying to show myself with a policeman in authority—I wait till I get to a higher authority, more on my level.

R.D.R.: Don't argue with the man who has a gun and a club.

A.B.: No sir, 'cause they're ignorant, that's why they put them out there.

R.D.R.: Let's speak a moment about Fats Navarro.

A.B.: He had a high voice and he spoke with a Southern accent and the way he pronounced words was the funniest thing. But he could turn around and write and speak perfect Spanish and wrote beautiful poetry in Spanish. I felt very bad about that, you know, the musicians deserted him when he got sick, they thought they'd catch tuberculosis. I always admired Miles for that, Miles was the only one who came, Miles and myself, and nursed him. He got so small, I don't know how much weight he lost, but he couldn't have been over 110 lbs. From 330, he dropped down to that. The reason was, the way Fats was raised, they believed in voodoo. They didn't even go to a dentist or nothin', they didn't believe in doctors. And when he did decide to go it was too late. He had T.B. a long time; he worked Billy Eckstine's band with tuberculosis. Everybody thought it was dope that was killing him. He started out as an alto saxophonist. He played tenor too—ho, ho, ho, you should have heard that. Between Gene Ammons and Dexter Gordon, he'd take the tenor sax and come out between them. His chops weren't up, but he could play; god, he could play. So many things about a lot of guys. Elvin Jones can play guitar and sing the Blues, the old Blues you like to hear.

R.D.R.: How do you feel about the commercialism many Jazz musicians are going after?

A.B.: Music is a talent, but it's a loan, just for a little while in life. Nature takes its course and the talent will be removed from you and handed over to somebody else. The talent belongs to the people and if you don't play, if you go for the money, you're going to lose your talent—you never find an armored car following a horse. The only thing that follows you to the cemetery is respect, so you got to make the choice. And are people going to disrespect you if you do one thing and then turn around and do something else? I don't blame them, I guess they had to do it.

R.D.R.: But they never come back the same.

A.B.: Yeah, well that's the price they have to pay. You have to make a choice, especially in this kind of music there's no turning around.

Bill Dixon

Bill Dixon was born on Nantucket Island, Massachusetts, in 1925, and moved to New York City in 1933. A renaissance man, Mr. Dixon is an accomplished educator and painter, and since the '60s has been one of the avant-garde's finest and most controversial figures. This, despite the fact that he has for the most part removed himself from "the scene" for lengthy periods of time, much of that time spent at Bennington College (since 1968) where he is currently chairman of the Black Music Department. Previous to this, Mr. Dixon held teaching posts at Ohio State University, George Washington University, University of Wisconsin, and Columbia. Between the '60s and '80s, Bill Dixon recorded infrequently; single albums under his leadership for Savoy and RCA and with Cecil Taylor for Blue Note account for most of this work. Since 1981, Mr. Dixon has released a series of outstanding recordings on the Italian Soul Note and Fore labels.

Through the years, Bill Dixon's relationship with the press has been stormy, a stand-off at best. He does not like to feel manipulated and cannot abide playing social and/or political "games." He is an existential man who believes you are what you are, not what you say you are. He also believes in as total a commitment as possible to the truth of one's stated purpose.

He is a fiercely independent individual and such people do not slide smoothly through a social system that depends on daily compromises—large or small, real or imagined. Also evident in Mr. Dixon is an element of anxiousness and suspicion which can bring on undue apprehensions of conspiracy and manipulation. Allowing for the position of the artist in the United States, particularly the uncomprising Black artist, the delineation between paranoia and reality is not particularly obvious.

In my adolescence I had been in awe of Paul Robeson and during my early adult years I had been similarly in awe of Bill Dixon. Bill Dixon was Bill Dixon, there was never any confusion or inconsistence in his pronouncements, verbal or musical. It was obvious to me Bill Dixon was playing to/for Bill Dixon and that is all we should ask of an artist.

Although I had interviewed former students and colleagues of Bill Dixon, I had never had any personal contact with him. I was aware his relationship with the press had been an adversary one and I knew he spurned (not always delicately) attempts to interview him; I'd been led to believe that he'd come to the conclusion that a relationship of noncooperation with the press was more beneficial (less negative and irritating) to him than one of cooperation. Basically I feel Mr. Dixon believes the press is really not as interested in listening to him as in molding their stories into what *they* want to hear.

In the fall of 1979, I received a message at the office that a William Dixon had called me and had asked me to return the call. It is not in my nature to return long distance phone calls to people I do not know. Usually it is some gratuitous call made at corporate expense either wanting something of you or wishing to engage you in the shallow insincere praise, hype, and backslapping which make up so much of what passes as friendship and business in the media. However, being both curious and ornery, I decided to return the call collect. The phone was answered and after charges were accepted, I introduced myself and the person on the other end said, "I want to comment on something that appeared in *Cadence* . . . ," and the person went on to elaborate quite articulately and knowledgeably on a particular matter. At which point I interrupted and asked whom I was speaking with. "This is Bill Dixon." "William Dixon, Bill Dixon, oh my god, BILL DIXON," I thought to myself as it finally dawned on me whom I was speaking to. The day the press called Bill Dixon collect and he accepted the call—an accomplishment which I would have never knowingly attempted. I have since taken to thoroughly analyzing names before returning calls.

Our phone relationship continued for a couple of years and the calls were often lengthy. During that time I repeatedly offered the forum of a *Cadence* interview to Mr. Dixon. Then one day in August 1981, he called and said he was ready for an interview. A week later he drove up to the Cadence Building and we spent a weekend together, relaxing, teasing each other, and every so often turning on the tape recorder and interviewing.

This interview is the only interview in this volume which I did not transcribe from tape to paper. It was transcribed by Kea Rusch.

R.D.R.: Am I right that this is the first interview you have consented to give in about fifteen years to any publication?

B.D.: It just might be. . . .It might be the first here, in terms of an in depth thing, with me discussing things and responding to questions put to me, in *this* country; it might be *the* first, because the only time I have had any documentation here was when I did, years ago (1967), something for *Coda Magazine* in Canada. But that wasn't an interview. I wrote that. As you also know, there is more of an interest in my work in Europe. Consequently, over the years, I have spoken at length to writers and journalists in Paris, Italy, Amsterdam, Vienna, London, Zurich and Scandinavia with the results that sometimes an interview, critique or sometimes an article of some significance has resulted. A year or so ago writer-critic Roger Riggins spent a week with me and, quite naturally, we engaged in a discussion that covered a wide range of interests. He, much to my surprise, assembled our talks into a rather interesting, I thought, article that he then presented to *Downbeat Magazine*. The severely truncated and edited version of Mr. Riggins' work that finally appeared in the magazine (and it wasn't a cover story because I was told over the telephone by an editor that because I don't do my work in this country, it wasn't possible for it to be a cover story) only served to distort and place out of context almost all that he and I had talked about.

R.D.R.: In the last half year there have appeared four Bill Dixon records, and now you're doing an interview.... Are you finally leaving your old Jazz Guild[1] or have conditions changed to your satisfaction?

B.D.: First of all, I don't think things have changed at all. I mean, true, there's a lot of activity, a lot of recordings, a reasonable amount of work, I would imagine, in New York, and places like that for certain musicians, because certain things have been resolved musically. Certain things are now in the air, they don't offer a certain kind of threat or rather anything like that to any of the so-called "establishments." They don't do that anymore. So we do have what we had years ago in a certain way. But, in a certain way, conceivably, it's worse. Myself, because I can't speak for anyone else really, I have started to think about, again, what is my next move. You know, one does something for a period of time and, so that you don't die, you have to do something else. And, as you know, I have made it a point to document things I've done about myself. The recordings, or what might be considered another kind of activity, is simply because there is something else that I want to do, and for whatever reason—it's been thought that I was either dead—for people who might have had some interest, and I have to now present a body of work for myself, to do the thing that I want to do, and to show certain things because I do have a plan. I am doing two things, so I'm going to tour more, not very extensively, because I'm not really interested in that. I'm going to record more, and I'm trying to get myself in a position so that I can release some things of mine that I think were important for me,

[1]The Jazz Guild was organized in 1964 by Bill Dixon to help protect and negotiate the interests of the New Music players of the time. Charter members included, among others, Sun Ra and Cecil Taylor.

that will also show myself, in proper perspective, in relationship to this music.

R.D.R.: The perspective that most people have of you has been one of a very angry person, a divisive person, and a hostile person. You are aware of that, right?

B.D.: Well, one can't be unaware of the perception that other people have of you. I mean, if you cut me, I'll bleed, and the blood is red just like anyone else's. I'm not unaware of any of the things that you're saying. I haven't been all of those things, certainly not all at the same time; really, although I do question the idea and assumption that being angry, especially after having emerged—not entirely unscathed—from some of the trying times and circumstances that one might find oneself in (and more especially if you've tried to do something that some people, who did wield some power, didn't want to acknowledge as being in existence—especially by you)—is necessarily either wrong or unhealthy. Who is to tell me that I must effect on my countenance a series of continuous smiles; why must it be thought or even suggested, at this point in time and history, that in order for me to *palatable*, that I must be cracking jokes and dancing *all* the time? Why is it that the people who've had considerable to do with *their* public and publicized version of *their* perception of me, feel that this can go on forever??

Eventually, the truth has to surface and a whole lot of people who have made contributions to this society in their chosen spheres of interest haven't necessarily been the "cup of tea" for everyone. But, I happen to know why they have been said, because I haven't been any of those things, really. It's very, very difficult. We're about two minutes into talking and something very, very important has surfaced. My perception of myself is, had I been White, an American, endowed with my gifts, and as a person who's involved himself in certain kinds of studies and a certain kind of activity, who's lived in certain places, in very important times, who has been able to see certain things in a certain way, and who has also tried to affect some kind of positive change for those things—I would be considered quite an honorable person. I mean, you would hear people speak of my tenacity, staying power, my driving a hard bargain, my being tough at the conference table. All of those things being viewed as the epitome of what we ascribe to American White males.

R.D.R.: It would be called integrity.

B.D.: It would be called integrity. Raising issues, or asking questions, and asking for definitive answers not soft shoe stepping, would be something that people could say, "Ah ha, we need more of that." The music business, which unfortunately I have to deal with at this particular time, and for the last 15 years, also the academic situation in America because I do teach, in certain instances they don't want to be questioned by an American Black male. Let me put it this way, they don't want to be questioned by an American Black heterosexual male. And, they're not going to and they don't have to. And they have the power at this particular time to resist your questions by trying to cast aspersions on your integrity.

R.D.R.: In the last 20 years, have you found a way to better control the results of whatever public relations do come out, good or bad? I mean, basically you seem to have just retreated from it.

B.D.: First of all, what someone says about you, and what you're doing, and when they try to make an interpretation of your intentions, has to be after you have done something. So, my feelings have been, I first have to do something, and my first concern, then in the past as it is now, is doing something. I cannot control what anyone is going to say about the results of that something.

Now, the small press that all of us get in this area of music—don't forget, we're not like the President where he can come in and have press conferences, and where you have all of these people raising their hands to eagerly speak to you and demand your attention—our so-called press situation is very, very miniature. We all know that to a certain degree, no matter how hostile any musician may be to this so-called press, for your work to reach the ears or the attention of any interested audience, this press has to be used. I was never the kind of the figure that, for what ever reason, this so-called press was interested in. I couldn't concern myself with that. What I have done instead is, I have very systematically done my work. I haven't been able to respond to the press because it would have been counter-productive for me to stop what I was doing, to even try to alert a public that might have been interested, that these things, in most instances, have nothing to do with what I was actually doing.

R.D.R.: I would like to say on the record because I don't think it's been said before, and I don't mean to dwell on your personality; my first perception of you, in the early '60s in NYC, was one of strength. After that point it was almost always negative. I saw you as a negative person, as a very divisive person, and as a picayune person. Now having talked to you for a couple of years I have never, never, once found you to be that way in reality or found you to be unreasonable. Or particularly pedantic. That doesn't mean I agree with you on everything.

B.D.: No, we don't have to agree. But, the interesting thing about what you are saying is I do have a personality pretty much the way anyone else does.

R.D.R.: You have a personality; not everybody *does* have a personality.

B.D.: No, I think everybody does, some people are not willing to show theirs. I have found that for myself, it's much more direct and less schizophrenic for me to be who I am.

R.D.R.: If you don't lie, you don't have to waste time covering your tracks.

B.D.: That's true. And you don't have to remember what you said in terms of what you "should" say to certain people.

R.D.R.: Well, there's only one thing you could say.

B.D.: That's right. The people who have been interested in what I do, have found it necessary and possible to come to where I am to hear what I do. They make that trip to Vermont, my concerts are always standing room only. I play for audiences that are just as large as any of the New York musicians'.

R.D.R.: Probably larger.

B.D.: Probably, more consistent. And there's one thing that's more important—I only do music that pleases me. I don't have to please anyone else, but myself.

R.D.R.: It could be more true; most people don't realize it to be more true than they believe it could be. You're near the Creative Music Studio, do you ever work there?

B.D.: I've had no association with them. Although I have given, upon occasion, students of mine, who wanted to go there to study, financial and moral support to go, and I have taught students who have studied there—that is they have come to Bennington to perform in ensembles of mine. I myself, I have never been invited to participate in any of those ventures.

R.D.R.: Is there more to this, or are we just going to feed the divisive fodder to follow it? (laughter)

B.D.: I don't know. (laughter) It might be that it's "difficult" to see me. I might be "difficult" to get a hold of. I'm chairman of the Department of Black Music, so obviously I spend a considerable amount of time in a place completely accessible. I might have a schedule that's much too "busy." My fee might be a bit "excessive." I mean, those are things the professional has to think about when he is obviously being excluded from participation in things that concern his field of interest.

R.D.R.: You also admit to not answering telephones or being available.

B.D.: When it serves my purpose, but I have a secretary.

R.D.R.: How does the October Revolution, two decades later, now look to you?

B.D.: Well, it's very interesting because this is a subject that is of infinite more importance to Europeans. They still discuss it as a *major* creative and social phenomenon. A lot of people who have gained incredibly, or immeasurably, from that situation have chosen, in certain ways, to denigrate the significance of that. A few years ago, there was an article in the *Villlage Voice* by a man (Gary Giddins) who writes for that paper, who appears to be articulate. He wrote a very extensive article, covering the development of the AACM, those people from Chicago. In passing, my name was mentioned as having done such and such and such. A colleague of mine, Steven Horenstein, who is also a writer, and who did his master's thesis on the suppression of certain areas in this music, called or wrote Mr. Giddins and said something about the article. And he (Giddins) said, "Well, Bill Dixon is really not of that much significance, and besides, his work and where he is, the locale, where he works, is far too remote." Now, the reason that I'm citing that—

R.D.R.: That's a NYC case of provincialism.

B.D.: That's right, of course. Now the same *Village Voice*, though, covers events in the theatre and does that rather thoroughly. In drama, the summer theatre situation at Williams College which is 20 minutes from where I am—going into Massachusetts. The point I'm trying to make is simply this, you have a situation, for whatever reason, where the work of certain people who were responsible, for *probably* the genesis of other people being completely negated. The October Revolution, was not designed to do anything at all except present some music in a set where the musicians could be comfortable and where an interested audience could come to see them at a price that they could afford. There were no far-reaching implications or ramifications intended; none of us had a crystal ball to know what was going to happen.

R.D.R.: I should just explain here, that the October Revolution was a series of concerts done in NYC in 1964, presenting new music.

B.D.: Presenting the music that the critical press, at the time, said in so many ways, overtly and subliminally, there were no audiences for and that it was anti-music to certain degrees that it was fascist music. But it *was* anti-Jazz, which is definitely what it was, although they didn't know really how accurate they were, because it was anti-Jazz certainly from a sociological point of view.

R.D.R.: Anti-Jazz life.

B.D.: That's right. So the thing about it was the people that participated in that situation have managed to become in certain ways part of the mainstream of what one might call Jazz music, and what some must call Black music.

R.D.R.: And have even in some cases gone on to playing mainstream music.

B.D.: Some have found it necessary to reverse themselves, for whatever reason. The thing is, the October Revolution was a very significant thing that happened and the thing that it produced after that, the Jazz Composers' Guild, whether people want to recognize it or not, allowed others entre for what we have now. The only reason the October Revolution was done, was because at the time I was thinking of opening my own place. I wanted to open my own place. I wanted a place where I could play whenever I wanted to.

R.D.R.: Did you have a name like the Dixon Line?

B.D.: No, the person that I was working with is still in N.Y. His name is Peter Sabino, who was a filmmaker, and he has a partner. They had this place on 91st Street, The Cellar, between Broadway and West End Avenue. At the time, I was living on 103rd Street, and after I finished my work, I was doing a lot of transcriptions of gospel music for Savoy and I'd walk the streets. One night I saw this place, went in there and struck up a friendship with these people. I came back from Savoy one day and stopped, I had some recordings of mine, I had the two things I had done for Savoy. They saw and played and liked them. And they made me then the musical director for The Cellar. We used to present Sunday afternoon concerts, which immediately were successful. I had one policy in directing that place. You could only play at The Cellar if they didn't let you play any place else. A lot of people played there, a very brilliant pianist, Valdo Williams. I don't know whatever happened to Valdo. There were several musicians, unfortunately their names have escaped me, who played up there. I used any instrumental combination I wanted to. I would occasionally give a concert. I remember using Joe Farrell—people like that—Dave Izenson, Charlie Moffet. When Rashid Ali first came to New York, he was my drummer. There were many, many, many people who played. It was a very, very beautiful time for me in my life. One night Peter and I were talking and I said, "Man, why don't we get a beer license here, and start to do something?" We started talking along those lines. We checked into it, we found it wasn't going to be that difficult. There was a woman that I knew who worked for the U.N. at that time, who had said to me when I worked there that if I ever wanted to make any kind of a venture, she would back me financially. So we started to make plans, and then we started to think of an opening for this. We were going to have an opening even before the thing was finalized. People said, yeah, let's have a big opening concert. One night we were thinking and talking and I said, "No, we shouldn't have a concert, man. We should have a week-long event." Now that was the genesis of the idea of this festival. We didn't want anyone with any kind of a name, we didn't want any support from anyone. And, if you notice, the original people who participated in the October Revolution were none of your original heavies even of that day in our underground.

R.D.R.: It wasn't Ornette?

B.D.: It wasn't Ornette. Cecil Taylor was also not invited to perform—

R.D.R.: Did you perform?

B.D.: Yes, I did. Archie Shepp was not invited to perform. They later, however, were invited to join the Jazz Composers' Guild, which was afterwards. What I did was—I got on the telephone, and I called musicians and said quite simply, "Listen, this is your chance to play, we're going to do this thing." And we had maybe 40 groups that came. There were some musicians who went from there to even greater obscurity—Giuseppi Logan, for example. Others, such as Milford Graves and John Tchicai went on to do something more public. Sun Ra had at that time an *excellent* band. He wasn't into his soft shoe about running the gamut of Fletcher Henderson, he wasn't doing that. In fact, at the time, I had in my possession two seven-inch tapes of an interview I did with Mr. Ra, for the now defunct Black literary magazine, *Umbra*. And we stayed on *this* planet. (laughter) So, the musicians came, and there was only one requirement. The musician played as long as he felt was necessary to make his point. To make it accessible to our public, we charged one dollar admission. Musicians or sidemen were paid something, leaders were paid nothing. That was because the leaders got all the glory. And the sidemen helped by participating in this enterprise and there was no reason for sidemen having to suffer economically. For example, if the group is a good group, the leader gets the credit. If the group is a bad group, the leader should share that responsibility. I'll never forget the day that it opened, we had all these candles because Con Ed had cut off the electricity. I mean, we made it into an event. It was supposed to start that afternoon. Opening time came. Nothing was happening when it was supposed to start anyway. So I went across the street, had a drink of beer. I forgot that I had anything to do... finally the phone rings. It's Peter Sabino on the phone, he says, "Bill, will you get over here right away!" I went downstairs, I saw this *mob*. Huh! I said, oh my god! Something has happened! I went in and the thing had started! And it was like that for four days and four nights. It was utterly fantastic. But there was no overt design to that.

R.D.R.: If there had been it probably wouldn't have come off because you would have had stars then. (laughs)

B.D.: Well, there's some things that just happen. Even the title, October Revolution. That was Peter Sabino's title. I think that's why people have tried to link me in certain kinds of ways with the kind of politics I've never really had anything to do with. He talked about the time it was happening and what the point was to be made, and we were doing it in October. It was his title.

R.D.R.: Did you find after that there was a different attitude on the part of the press? Did it frighten them or concern them?

B.D.: Well, the interesting thing about that series was, a considerable number of club owners from all over the city came to those concerts. Your critical establishment type also came. It was acknowledged in print in an issue of *Downbeat Magazine* by both Morganstern and Williams that I had proved my point that there was an audience for this music. One night, weeks later, Dan Morganstern showed up with a couple of musicians who had defected from a Russian ensemble, and people from the State Department. One of the first places the musicians had wanted to come to was The Cellar, and I was introduced to them. A certain kind of credibility had sort of been established. There were, however, rumblings starting to happen, because it was almost as though the natives were getting restless. They are going to ask for more.

R.D.R.: It's also usually a signal for people to somehow get in and exploit it and start to control it.

B.D.: Well, there was a person who did it right away. The person who ended up with ESP Records.

R.D.R.: Stollman.

B.D.: Bernard Stollman, who at the time, and I don't know if this has been documented, was the attorney for Cecil Taylor and Ornette Coleman. You can't exploit anything unless you have a person who wants to be exploited. The Institution of Slavery, in fact, involved a tacit agreement between one who was going to enslave and be responsible for that, and the other one who was going to be enslaved.

R.D.R.: Some of the more militant spokesmen, or some of the bigger mouths of the period, it seems to me, allowed themselves to be the most exploited.

B.D.: People were begging for exploitation. You have to be exploited in order for you, if you have any kind of thing that you want to do at all, to make it so you can escape the horrible thing that allowing yourself to be exploited will do, if you can surface from that—If someone came to me and said, "Listen, I have five million dollars, would you make a disco recording?" I would make the best god-damned one so fast because I would never have to do it again. Most people being exploited, they get what you would call *not even a bacon and eggs* kind of situation. So we have people speaking very eloquently, and articulately, and also being allowed to speak on certain issues, who although they were speaking and speaking very accurately to these issues their lives and how they live them makes their utterances of things profound ring hollow. In other words, in the way and manner that they were orienting their lives to get somewhere, they made lies of these words. That's why they were allowed to speak. A lot of musicians, of this period, for whatever reason, later sought to retrace their musical steps. There are a couple now who are considered very, very important now that they are now able to play things and incorporate those previously established things into their music. But, formerly they either couldn't do, didn't want to do or sneered at that.

R.D.R.: Now it's called the tradition.

B.D.: Now it's called the tradition. We now have this business where running the range of musical expression for certain Jazz players, is supposed to be the epitome of performance. Where we would never tolerate that in so-called classical or concert music. We don't want a person playing a piece by Palestrina, a piece by Correlli, Beethoven. We don't want that from people, we want to know their musical identification. In this music, we had a situation where certain things happened for certain musicians, because the person who was documenting these things, in terms of events and your historian and your critic, saw fit to deal with people that he had some kind of special, or social relationship with, or vested interest in a certain kind of way. So that certain things that happened in terms of the music, your public would never have known anything about, had they been solely dependent on these people for the information.

R.D.R.: Any recording from those Cellar days?

B.D.: When we did the four days in the December series at Judson Hall, I hired Jerry Newman. But, no members of the Guild wanted their works recorded, but when Jerry Newman showed up, they did make separate agreements with him to record theirs. The fact that a wider public, interested in this music, might not know was because even your critical establishment—who should be charged with a responsibility the way they are charged with a responsibility in painting and in literature—didn't have to be. They spoke of the work and reviewed the work and did essays on the work of the people that they could tell you that they were interested in.

R.D.R.: A lot of the press is made up of glorified fans.

B.D.: They really are. A man collects records for 20 years... when he has a large enough collection, he writes a liner note, he becomes a critic. I can cite you the instance of a well known musician-writer-critic who was having breakfast one Sunday morning at my house during the early '60s. He was lamenting the fact that he had to write an article on a person that he had done several on previously. I had, at the time, very little documented on my work. This is in New York and I'm not unaware of the power of the printed page. I said to him I could certainly use an article. He looked me right in the eye and said, "Well, man, I write on the people I dig." So you had this kind of situation, you have this kind of situation now. There is a reason for the endless plethora of interviews or articles on a Sun Ra, or on an Archie Shepp, or on a Cecil Taylor and it has less to do with the perceived significance of their work than it does with other things. But, one does have to come to terms on some level with him.

R.D.R.: I can't pass this by, you were called a painter manqué right?

B.D.: Yes, right.

R.D.R.: You don't want to elaborate on this, right?

B.D.: Well, the interesting thing about that, that title was given to me by Dan Morgenstern and it appeared in a very handsome book of photographs. I think the photographer was Danish.

R.D.R.: Yes, Ole Brask.

B.D.: This book was published by the Harry Abrams people, who publish these magnificent books on painting, on contemporary painters. At one time the Abrams firm was interested in a book on the collaborative work of Judith Dunn and myself. This is again something that is not known. Anyway, this book (*Jazz People,* by Brask and Morgenstern) really says nothing about me, but my name is mentioned when they discuss Archie Shepp and his early work and in making that reference, Morgenstern, the same Dan Morgenstern who is now Director of the Institute of Jazz Studies at Rutgers, refers to the fact that Archie and I co-led a group and also says that "Bill Dixon who was a painter manqué, who also at the time talked a bigger game than he can play." So we would have to define. But because what he did was, he didn't seem to understand a painter manqué, the social significance of *him* labeling me, which meant a failed painter, a person who hasn't succeeded financially, since to my knowledge he never saw a painting of mine, or if I hadn't succeeded within the world of painting which at the time, as you know, was completely antagonistic, and hostile to Black painters and dominated by Whites.

R.D.R.: It's incredible to me that a critic of the arts could use the term a painter manqué, especially about painting. I don't understand what Dan could have meant.

B.D.: As a critic he has a perfect right to say whatever he wants relating to facts that *he* knew if he had said, "Well, his painting was absolutely terrible..."

R.D.R.: Right, that's really different.

B.D.: That's quite different. Or, "His painting didn't appeal to me because..."

R.D.R.: Which is the most accurate.

B.D.: Which is the most accurate. Or, "I never saw any of his paintings." But I have to assume that he felt that because my name never appeared at the Castelli Gallery and things like that he would have to feel that I evidently couldn't have been a painter of any substance. But then if you were speaking of a Black painter in the early '60s, you had to understand the Pandora's box that can be opened here, which conceivably could point to the social conditions and your insensitivity and where were *you* when they were denying those Black painters entrée to shows, which only started to happen when painters, of merit from the Black community with White support began to question the kinds of shows that were being mounted under the aegis of American painting, at the same time excluding the significant Black painters. That's what makes that kind of thing interesting. That points to a certain kind of "critical assessment" of values and history which also points to how vulnerable those people were and still are, and how they could become very vindictive, and try to do things to you if you questioned them, or sought to raise issues because in certain ways you needed them.

R.D.R.: Well, that's the thing. I'm not equating what we're doing with what you have achieved. But *Cadence* is also *not popular* particularly in New York City.

B.D.: That's one of the best things that can happen for you.

R.D.R.: They just can't reach us. We're just not dependent on the whole thing. I think for a while they hoped we would go away. And they assumed we would.

B.D.: That's right.

R.D.R.: And here we are six years later and we seem to be getting stronger and "better." We have heard stories.

B.D.: Survival is your only defense and the final insult is death. So one can't even die. You've got to fight. If that car hits you at 90 miles an hour, you have *got* to get up.

"He talked a better game than he could play." What does that mean? By whose standards! Did Stravinsky "talk a better game than he could play" before his work was made more accessible to the interested listening public? Did Schoenberg "talk a better game than he could play" when he was both critical of the acceptance that both Bartok and Stravinsky were getting at what he felt was at his partial expense?

R.D.R.: You've come a long way from a manqué. (laughter)

B.D.: Well, speaking of that, incidentally, it's very, very interesting, because in June of 1982, I will have a show of my paintings and do a solo concert, and give a lecture on esthetics and philosophy of Black music in Verona (Italy).

The point to be made is—we were speaking about references to the negative attitude of my countenance that had been postulated in such a way that people had considered me a troublemaker. And an agitator. Even if they could, in the deeper senses of their minds, say "He is speaking of something that's very important, but look how he's doing it."

R.D.R.: There are certain things that should be made trouble.

B.D.: Well, it is to be hoped. When I was down in Tallahassee (Florida) at this Cannonball Adderley festival, after I came back from London last year (1980), I didn't perform. I was invited to give two talks. We discussed the things that are generally discussed in universities: social ramifications; artistic ramifications of the music, and things like that. This was before a small audience. Later on, the woman who invited me, Pamela something, I can't remember the name, related something to me that was rather curious. This is a Black woman who was running this thing. She said, when I did accept coming down there, she was rather elated, because I haven't done much of this activity outside of my own school. So she said she'd called another person, Martin Williams, who's the director of the Smithsonian Jazz section there, and asked him if he would want to come down and be on the panel. He asked who was going to be on it. She said, "Well, Bill Dixon from Bennington, Vermont." She said to me, he said he "did not want to be on any panel with any Marxist avant-garde musician." Which again, could prompt one to say, come on now Bill, I just don't believe Mr. Williams would say that about you. Or, why would he say something like that about you. The fact is, it was said.

R.D.R.: If you say it and someone believes you, then it puts certain aspersions on your troublemaking and puts the focus where it doesn't belong, instead of on why the trouble should be made.

B.D.: It takes a whole lot of moxie for a person to cite what he considers to be your political beliefs or political stance, based solely on your record of not taking crap from people.

R.D.R.: It doesn't relate to the artistry...

B.D.: It doesn't relate to the issues. But again, this is relating to the fact that whatever I did when I was in New York which had something to do with bringing attention to the dilemma of the music at the time, and its noncritical acceptance, and the fact that these people were not willing to present to interested listeners an unbiased view of the musical happenings that were taking place in New York City which at the time was considered to be the high point of artistic activity. I become then, a person who talked, again, "a better game than he could play." We've always had this mystique about the Jazz musician. He was like a one-celled amoeba, he could only play and please you, he did nothing else, he certainly didn't do any thinking or questioning. When he stepped out of that role, then he was persona non grata. We have never tolerated that idea in formal concert music.

R.D.R.: Are there musicians out of the October Revolution Era who you feel have been true to a certain artistic and social integrity?

B.D.: It is very interesting to me now to see some of the people who were then the most "honest" that now are becoming extremely utilitarian. Now saying things like, "There could never be art for art's sake, it's about the people and the workers" and this and that, and "the music and people have to dance" and, "I have to change what I'm doing now to get to that little girl there on the corner who wouldn't listen to me before." Mind you, mine is naturally a miniaturist point of view and it is naturally quite biased. I haven't heard that many musicians that I once spent time with sticking to the premise of doing what they did because that was a primary necessity, and a responsibility, if they were to call themselves creative people. A lot of them have been extremely successful, not in terms of what they may have gotten in terms of money. So this one may own a little farm, etc. The interesting thing is, when you die everyone goes into the ground. When you ask me that question, I am compelled to answer that whether I want to or not, I am forced to be aware of what's happening musically because I teach and I have to present to my students a body of unbiased information. I can't teach as a critic, and I think I do my teaching as a professional very well and sometimes under duress, because I find myself having to teach about people that I no longer have any kind of interest in and very little respect for some of the things they do musically and socially. So many musicians will say to you, "Well, I'm doing this, man, because like I don't wanna lay too much stuff out there man, because if I put this out there then I can sneak in a little of this."

R.D.R.: But how do you answer someone who says to you, "That's easy for you to say, Dixon, you went off and disappeared into the academic world, but I don't have that kind of intellectual ability, or that acceptance, and I'm still out here doing what I know how to do best and I have to live and try to combine the two"?

B.D.: I've prepared myself for what I was going to do. That's what I tell these doggone so-called street cats. There was a very interesting thing in Valerie Wilmer's book, where a musician, a very, very good bass player who, based on his own kind of ability to function in a certain kind of way, I once made accessible to him and a group of people to come up to the college and perform for a couple of days. This man couldn't even find his way to the Greyhound bus station and therefore never got there and when he was interviewed in Valerie Wilmer's book—talking about, "Yeah, some of our best cats are going into these universities and teaching. . ." it comes off as a joke. The rhetoric is as big as this land around here, because let me tell you something, my phone rings all the time from all of these cats who, if they could, they would like to be doing that. But they did not think it was significant years ago for them to do anything but talk about the minimal thing they did. I spent an incredible amount of time preparing myself for my move. Doing the kinds of studies that people were then sneering at. I was dealing with music that they like to call World music now and things like that, long before they were popular. As a study for information.

R.D.R.: You were born and grew up, I believe, in Nantucket.

B.D.: That's true.

R.D.R.: Okay, you had family background which had a certain sense for education, in the formal sense, an importance for it. You were brought up in surroundings that were not typical, I think.

B.D.: I was about eight when I came to New York. And, you forget, I grew up in New York at the height of the Depression. I was born in 1925, my family moved to New York in 1934, so I was nine years old. When we first moved to New York, I was the first of the children in my family who, because of being humiliated in school about the way we spoke, worked very hard to speak without a Boston accent, which we had. It was very, very rough growing up in New York during the Depression. I have two brothers and two sisters. My first responsibilities were taking care of my brothers and sisters. I have been working and self-sufficient as an individual since I was 14 years old. I worked my way through school—there were no grants for you as a "human being" then; there were no NEH grants; there were no Guggenheims; there were no CAPS grants for storefront art. There was no kind of anything. When I went to Frederic Douglass Jr. High School, (PS 139, N.Y.C.), it was during the time of the street gangs, you couldn't go into this block without getting your behind kicked. On Nantucket, my family was a very secure family, a highly respected family. When I was there as a kid there might have been 25 to 30 families on that island during the winter. When I came to New York, I had never seen so many damned people in my life, let alone Black people. One of the first things that happened to me when I came to New York, I went to the store and I was robbed, I was robbed by a man who later became a *very*, very good drummer. I used to get beaten up in school, we were made fun of because of the way we spoke, and the way we carried ourselves. So it wasn't this panacea, a lot of people tried to act as though I invented my circumstance from outside. I invented my circumstance from inside.

R.D.R.: I think the compromise should be as consciously minimal as whatever's possible. For many people it's consciously more than it would have to be.

B.D.: It's funny, you using that term, I had a talk this summer in Italy, we talked for two days about this. The older that I get, the more I feel I'm really right. I'm going to be 56 on my next birthday. My premise is if you are right, and everyone knows that you are right, I don't believe a compromise is possible. It's different if they don't believe or acknowledge that you are right. Okay, so then you've got to find a way to continue. If it's acknowledged that you are right, it is, therefore, impossible to make a certain kind of compromise. What we have here is an art form of significance that happened in this country and affects the world, it's a Black art. We don't know why it happened here, we know that it happened here, and we know that it has been a thing that has affected musical change throughout the world, sometimes more subliminally than overtly. We know also because of the social structure of this country, the person who has made the invention that everyone could benefit from is still not being given his due in certain kinds of ways. Your query now will be, and the question is classic, "Well, can't a White person play Jazz?" That's not what I'm talking about. That's another chapter. The other thing, because the vestiges of slavery must've been so pervasive—what conceivably could be the ramifications really of a people held in bondage, for the amount of years that Black people have been held in bondage in this country. Jumping very, very fast, Black musicians for the most part, under the guise of using this thing called survival are merely reflecting what must have been an incredibly traumatic experience. Acknowledge that if you do this music, why can't you be part of the decision-making process, why can't you get more, why is it that an entrepreneur can have in his house a ten foot Steinway grand, and you're lucky if you have a Yamaha upright! But if you behaved yourself (you're told and not so subliminally), maybe a company might have loaned you one for an unlimited amount of time? Why is it so great then for you to work for scale when like maybe an agent has a summer home or something? So, I understand these things, I'm not impervious to the fact that every musician cannot function the same way every person can. I can't run a four-minute mile, although it's documented in the books, man has run a four-minute mile.

Time is running out for us in our petty idiosyncratic behavior towards just getting along. We Black people don't have all this time left anymore to get our heads together. Or as one major musician said to me when we were getting ready to go to Europe, for our first European tour in 1962, when this man showed up at my house eight hours late for rehearsal after having called me repeatedly on the hour when he was getting in the subway here, getting in the subway there—"The man has got our minds fucked up!!!" Knowing all this, I find it highly offensive when people say to me, "But Bill, *you* are exceptional, you have the security of a teaching job." They would not have survived what I have had to do on my teaching job to keep that integrity. So, we can say this, this is very dangerous what I'm going to say now, but I'm going to say it. Perhaps there is an iota of truth when it is alluded to that certain cats are never going to have it together. Genetically, maybe they only can play these horns. Do you understand that?

R.D.R.: Well, I—

B.D.: Well, no, you can't say that, I can.

R.D.R.: Well, I don't agree with that.

B.D.: I don't agree with it. I'm saying though, in pursuit of reasons for certain things, you have to examine as many of the variables, and then you have to deduce so that you come to a conclusion. This is now a form of instant replay, it is incumbent upon us now to stop the bullshit, stop talking the omnipresent they, *look what* **they** *have made me do, look at what* **they** *are making me do. I have got to pay my rent, because I'm more important than you . . .*

R.D.R.: Okay, I hear you, but what you're talking about now is just self-respect.

B.D.: I think primarily, it has to do with how you do ultimately feel about yourself and what for you is the bottom line.

R.D.R.: But on the other hand, as you said, not everyone can run the four-minute mile.

B.D.: And I understand that.

R.D.R.: I agree with that and I feel as a devil's advocate, saying the other thing, because people will use that for an excuse to say *he's just special.*

B.D.: Yeah, he drives a foreign car. You know how I bought my car—

R.D.R.: (laughter) Oh, I've really got him going now.

B.D.: No, I used to get these dumb, little $25-$35, $3.92 royalty checks. I used to feel terrible about taking these into the bank, a big time composer cat, so one day I put it in the goddamned drawer, to hell with it! One day, I opened the drawer, there was all of this paper. Now dumb as I was, I didn't know you're supposed to cash a check before 90 days, they can cancel the damn thing. As providence would have it the sages were in my favor. I went to the bank, I had four thousand dollars in these damned little things. So I just put them away. I was a composer in residence one summer at George Washington University and I walked down the street and I saw this incredible car. I live in New York, what are you going to do with a car? I didn't know a car from a truck. That car so attracted me that I never got to teach my class that day. And I just looked at this car, I had never seen a thing that looked—I just loved it. But I didn't know what it was, so I got back to New York, I started looking in magazines, (laughs) it was a Corvette sting ray. It was simply beautiful. So I began to read about it, you know, read, read, read...

R.D.R.: It wasn't purple was it?

B.D.: No, it was electric blue. (laughter) To make a long story short, I, one day, wanted to buy it and I withdrew some money and I went and put 500 dollars down on this car, on 57th St. As I walked out of the building, an XKE passed and I said, "Oh, my god!" I ran in and got my money back. I said to my son "That's the one!" Well, I looked at that car. I rubbernecked, I just looked, and looked, and looked. I went crazy because I couldn't afford it. I lived in N.Y. and I used to teach summers at Columbia University Teacher's College. One summer went very badly, one day I didn't know what to do. I got in a taxi coming from Columbia driving downtown. I lived down on 13th Street, and I told the man to drive through the park. I'm sure he thought I was trying to rob him or something, because he kept looking at me funny. So finally, I said take me to Madison Avenue, 57th Street. I went in there, wrote a check and I ordered my car. Then the sense of exhilaration—because I had to order mine. I was going to have to wait, right. I then went to a driving school. I learned how to do the sports car thing. And it's funny, when I got the car, because then I went to a bank in Vermont and they gave me the rest of the money, the first time that I drove that car on campus, a man jumped out, who was director of development. He said, "How did you get it, did you get a grant?" No one would assume that you could want something, and I didn't want a Volkswagen, I didn't want a Ford, and I would be willing to have nothing until I had that. It's the only car I have ever owned and musicians used to see me driving that fuckin' car and it reaffirmed their opinion of me. "That's why you can do the music that you want, because you don't have to do this." And everyone really knows now that's not true.

R.D.R.: I don't think everyone does know that, Bill. What would you say about a musician who missed a class, a gig, or a plane because of a blue Corvette?

B.D.: Well, if he was the leader of the group, that's his business. He's only hurting himself, that's all, because if he misses that plane, he's still responsible for those people being paid for that day. But I worked, and I don't compromise. I don't! And mind you, I can be just as frustrated as anybody else. But that's my business. I don't carry it into my job and into my work. I used to wreck the furniture in my house until I realized I couldn't afford that, and it was self-defeating. I have worked hard trying to maintain my sanity, mental and physical health in that order.

As I was discussing with you last night, I think every person who does something special and significant does it because of a desire to let others really know you as well. So there can be no problem with them really knowing you. Sometimes your work speaks more eloquently about certain things about you than anything else; it can give a person a clue. I really don't do my work for anyone except myself. I would have done what I did if I'd been a millionaire ten times over. It would be *really* incredible if everything you did could be perceived by people for the reasons that you did it. But you can't, so then what you have to do is you have to forget all of these things. You have to forget; here's a guy who reviews a record of yours, he completely misses your intention. When you're 22, you can write your letter to the editor. At 32, you can't write that letter. At 55, it's taking you away from what you do. I'm getting old enough to finally understand that.

R.D.R.: It's amazing how precious time becomes.

B.D.: The older you get.

R.D.R.: If you just get down to the business of doing it, one day you'll blink your eyes and see what you achieved.

B.D.: True. With a great deal of regularity I can feel that I have done something that day. I can't waste any more time, because even if I cross with the green and not in between I'm not going to be here another 50 years. (laughter) Well, it's true, some people act as though they have the secret about living forever.

R.D.R.: Are you conscious of any so-called trumpet influences on you?

B.D.: Well, now, you're the first person who has really asked me that. The first person I ever heard play the trumpet, and this should be interesting, was Louis Armstrong. I heard him the first year we came to New York.

R.D.R.: Fronting a prominent big band.

B.D.: That's right. I think it was Don Redman's band.

R.D.R.: Luis Russell?

B.D.: Luis Russell, O.K.

My stepfather took me to hear Louis Armstrong at the Lafayette Theatre in Harlem. We sat upstairs, and my stepfather was a big man, he was six feet two or three, big man. There were four or three trumpets, they had the whole big band set up and everything. This one man came out and played and I can remember to this day. He played like I had never heard anything like that in my life, because he played all over all those cats. On my way home that night, I said to my stepfather, "I want one of these." I didn't get it. When I was a teenager, the first trumpet player that I heard *as* a trumpet player who had a remarkable affect on my thinking about the instrument from a technical standpoint, and this may shock you, was Harry James. "Carnival of Venice," "Flight of the Bumblebee," pieces like that, I love those pieces. The person who had a profound thing in terms of how he played, and the sound that he took out of Horn, was Rex Stewart. And mind you now, I heard Rex Stewart at the dances we went to as a teenager because the Ellington band, the Lunceford band, all of those, they played for our dances, I heard them *live*. And you could sit down there man, and just dig those cats playing. So, you were talking about influences and I want to get to Miles Davis.

R.D.R.: I'll bet you do.

B.D.: When I started to play the horn, when I started to study, don't forget, the person who was absolutely terrifying on the horn at that time was Dizzy. I also heard him with Earl Hines. But, it's funny, you didn't have to know who it was because he did something with the music that was different. When I first heard the records of he and Bird, hey, I wept. In those days, don't forget, Louis was "old hat." But Dizzy, it was impossible to escape the force that Dizzy had on that horn, in terms of completely eliminating all of the things that had made the trumpet previously just a clarion-sounding instrument. I first heard Miles Davis play at the Three Deuces, which was on 52nd Street and you could stand up on this sidewalk, and the bandstand faced you and you could listen. One night, Bird didn't show up. Now trumpet players with quartets, I mean like say trumpet with a rhythm section; all right, so Lips Page had done it and things like that. But it was really quite a formidable task and Little Miles Davis was playing—goddamn, who is this cat?! No one knows why ultimately he took the stance on the instrument that he did. We don't know if it was accident, if he sat down and decided after so many years, we don't know what he did, and strangely enough, no one has ever asked him. But we know his approach to the horn in terms of the sound. And he brought to the instrument, to my ear, one of the most beautiful sounds I have heard come out of the trumpet.

R.D.R.: Sometimes your orchestrations sound almost like orchestrations of Miles Davis, I don't mean to take anything away from you.

B.D.: No, I wouldn't be upset about that because—

R.D.R.: Well, I'm talking just about sound, I'm not talking about composition. I mean it's something you use as part of your composition because compositions are so much more than just orchestrations of Miles Davis. It's an element of it.

B.D.: That's true. I listened very, very carefully to almost everything that he did. I'm telling you this and no one's ever heard this. And one time I could play note for note every solo that he had. However, when one has used up all that one needs, and it's no longer necessary for you to be either dependent, influenced, anything—and you become then who you are. And you have absolutely nothing to do with it, you cannot say you're going to be an individual.

R.D.R.: It's like the October Revolution.

B.D.: That's right. It's the same premise. One day, and I don't know when it first started to happen, I started to point myself on the instrument. I think that started to happen to me around 1960.

R.D.R.: Relatively late.

B.D.: Very late. But don't forget I came to music very late.

R.D.R.: Well, very late for then; I think people are now coming into their own later.

B.D.: Yeah, but you know I didn't even start to study then, till I was 20, going on 21. And, I made my first recording then when I was 37.

R.D.R.: It was just about your last recording.

B.D.: Almost. (laughter) First and last. I think if you play a record of Miles Davis', I still think you can hear in the work, and I don't know, it could also be reversed too, certain affinities in the way sound is dealt with in certain kinds of ways. I've never discussed it with him, I'm sending him that set (two releases on the Italian Fore label) of recordings. I don't think anyone listening would hear anything, aside from a certain attitude in Miles Davis' work. You could've said he and I shared the same affinity for a quality of sound.

R.D.R.: Color.

B.D.: A kind of coloristic kind of thing.

R.D.R.: Did you like Chet Baker during the '60s at all?

B.D.: Well, you know, it's funny—I saw Chet Baker and spent some time with him last year in Paris. Chet Baker was playing in a place not too far from me. I hadn't seen him or heard him in years. He played absolutely beautifully, he always had a certain kind of control.

R.D.R.: And he's matured.

B.D.: Well if you go through the stuff that certain people go through and you don't grow up—

R.D.R.: You die.

B.D.: —that's right, you die. The thing about it was during the time that he was playing, I listened very intently to that Mulligan quartet that he was with. Which I thought the group still sustains itself very, very well, really. And there were some things that I thought Ted Curson did which were good. Cecil had a group at one time, late '50s, with Ted Curson and Bill Barron. They worked one job as far as I knew, at the Village Gate, and they rehearsed maybe a year—everyday. Bobby Bradford, when he first came after Cherry, I thought Bobby was an incredibly beautiful player. There was no hurry in his work. During the '50s, I also happened to be a person who really dug Bobby Hackett (laughs). You know what I mean, playing those Gleason songs and stuff.

One is influenced by everything. There are certain things you can't say that's not going to affect you.

R.D.R.: You passed over one trumpeter which is surprising, Art Farmer.

B.D.: Art played so beautifully, I happen to like his work... But, to change the subject a bit, I don't think that the (trumpet) players have dealt with the next move on the trumpet. I hear a lot of players, and I see a refinement with an occasional, what might be called "left wing excursion" to what they think is where it should be. The trumpet has been freed a long time ago from its allegiance to what was considered its literature. The trumpet is as flexible as the violin. Once you adopt that stance, however, you eliminate from your repertoire any of the old music. And, if you're going to play with other people, you've still got to be able to address yourself to that. So you hear trumpet players now, and almost all of them are good, they are technically much better than when I was starting to play because the new music hadn't been that fully codified, there wasn't that much to study. But, very few of them have the imagination that trumpet players had when I was starting to study.

R.D.R.: Do you think of yourself as a father of the avant-garde?

B.D.: No.

R.D.R.: . . . A legend in your own time?

B.D.: Yes.

R.D.R.: Do you enjoy being a legend in your own time?

B.D.: Yes, of course. But, the funny thing about someone calling you anything is, I can remember when World War II ended in Germany. I was in Germany. We would go to various places and signs would read: "Kilroy was here," and we never knew who Kilroy was. I have felt sometimes like Kilroy, especially in Europe, and I would meet people and there were very few books where my name isn't mentioned in a certain kind of way. But I have met people who thought I was like a Kilroy (laughter), that I really did not exist. It's really rather interesting. I know that in certain ways my work has been acknowledged. I intended only to be in music, because I love music, that's why I studied music. I had no intentions originally to become a musician. Music is something that you can hear and can't see. I used to be fascinated by looking at a piece of manuscript paper. But you study, before you know it you're doing it.

R.D.R.: You sort of fall into it.

B.D.: The term avant-garde, what was the term we used. We knew we were doing music. I think we preferred—

R.D.R.: New Music, Free Jazz?

B.D.: No, New Music was always the term. I mean everything has its own discipline.

R.D.R.: Oh, I agree. Technically what's it mean, except that it became a standard version?

B.D.: I do think in retrospect that the term, New Music, was more appropriate, because I can remember when Dizzy's music and their music was called New Music. And I think that was the term that made us feel rather proud, because I go back to the time when I was very, very proud to be a Jazz musician because I didn't want to be one of the other musicians. The translation process of how one feels about one's self is an evolutionary process. The New Music was something we did. When I was in New York in the late '50s, up to the middle '60s, you were there too, it was an extremely exciting place to be there.

R.D.R.: Yes, but you didn't realize, I mean you knew, but you didn't really know and you look back and say, "Wow!"

B.D.: Everything was breaking out and making something else. There was modern dance, painting was very exciting and mixed media, whatever. We used to go to the new foreign films.

R.D.R.: Yeah, and you look back and they weren't so dumb.

B.D.: No, they were not. We would on Sundays if I had done something to get money, have breakfast at O'Henry's on Sixth Avenue in the village and read the *Sunday Times,* it was really quite a collective period. Plus, there wasn't as much hostility in New York, I mean I lived on Bank Street, man you could be in the street at 3:00 or 4:00 in the morning. Cecil Taylor and I used to sit up Sheridan Square talking about music, watch the sun come up.

R.D.R.: All you had to do was watch out for the police, that was basically it. (laughs)

B.D.: They were the cats.

R.D.R.: They were!

B.D.: I mean I see these guys playing music, now, you couldn't play any music in Washington Square Park, unless it was folk music or the Italians playing their kind of mandolin choir music, and things like that. It was a time of extreme productivity, and we knew we were not within the mainstream. The most we could hope for, was get a Sunday afternoon at the Five Spot. Or Monday night, that was a black night anyway. The coffee house was really our saving grace, because the coffee houses at that time, the late '50s, were really beautiful as a phenomenon, because they paid you so little money they didn't care what you played.

R.D.R.: There was also an apartment scene too, like the loft scene except they weren't lofts, they were apartments. What do you think of the loft scene? It was over when it was recognized.

B.D.: Once they started calling it the loft scene it was doomed because how can one make oneself a subculture overtly? I think the thing that irritated me the most about the touted loft scene of recent years was that all of these musicians displayed a kind of musical and historical arrogance and lack of sophistication concerning anything that had come before them, and a way of posturing about being able to do the best of everything. It was really very offensive.

R.D.R.: But, you know I remember during the '60s getting that impression from the New Music players.

B.D.: It was because the players that came to what was then the New Music, knew that there was no way in the world, the way things existed, for you to become a part of the then real music establishment. Because, the people who were then a part, had just become a part themselves, and they weren't about to give one inch, you know. I think everyone had more love of the music than now. Economics weren't that much discussed. Don't forget, no one was being interviewed. The Jazz Composers' Guild and the October Revolution, we couldn't even get people to review us, there was none of that. So our thing was different. Now, when I look back, there was a lot of musical activity. I remember George Russell rehearsing right next door to me. I would be rehearsing. Lamont Young was in my building, Lamont would be doing something. Down the corner John Benson Brooks would be rehearsing. Freddie Redd... There was a lot of activity but no one really, I think, consciously thought of himself outside of the area of where you were doing the music. This is what you had to do, there was nothing else you could do.

R.D.R.: There was bitching and moaning, but that was part of the condition.

B.D.: Now man, these people get so much publicity. They produce so many records and I think what has bothered me more than anything else has been the fact that because they have learned to play some Ellington songs, that is supposed to place them out there in a certain kind of way. I don't believe in it. . . . What is this that makes the musicians think that they have got to be able to make themselves accessible to everyone. This is what I hear all the time. I read a whole lot about these cats from Chicago. I met David Murray. I was very prepared to dislike him, because I felt that at his age he had too many records. I met him in Florence; he's a gentleman. "Hello, Bill, I'm David Murray." He came up to me, said he recognized me from my pictures. I didn't know him, I'd never seen him. When David Murray came to a concert of mine we stayed in the same hotel and to me he displayed himself as a gentleman.

R.D.R.: You do music, your paintings are quite lovely considering you're a manqué—

B.D.: Exactly, I'm a painter manqué. (laughter) (See page 135.)

R.D.R.: And, I've also read a very short portion of your autobiography which is very much like your music, not particularly like your paintings, I don't see the connection there but I could relate it to your music. Is this book coming out?

B.D.: Which book?

R.D.R.: Your autobiography.

B.D.: Oh, that book. I'm not really sure. If I had my way, I would like to do all these things myself. I would like to have the resources, to be able to do it myself. I'm not really that interested in, and there's probably not too many people that are interested in, an autobiography of Bill Dixon. Let's face it, it sounds incredibly egotistical *per se* to think that that could happen. But, for me though, as a part of my work for the last 15 years, I've been working on three books.

R.D.R.: What are the three books?

B.D.: The three books I've been working on are a history of the music from the '60s, the period where I became significant to myself as a musician. I've been working on my autobiography and that stems from letters and a journal that I used to keep.

And, I've also been working on a theoretical analysis of 20th century practices as they relate to this music. These are very serious ventures for me, I'm not a writer, so writing is a rather laborious enterprise.

R.D.R.: I was wondering if it upset you that you were not included in the latest edition of the *Encyclopedia of Jazz?*

B.D.: Well, not really, no.

R.D.R.: That wasn't your choice?

B.D.: Well, it's never one's choice.

R.D.R.: Oh, some people didn't want to be included and he respected that.

B.D.: I think that's true. I had to look at it from this standpoint, I have been extremely adamant about vocally representing myself as not being a Jazz musician. It seemed to me that because it was drawn to my attention that I was not included in an encyclopedia on Jazz, it would be rather hypocritical of me to be complaining about it. I'm not a Jazz musician, why should I be included in an encyclopedia on things that pertain to a thing that I say I'm not.

R.D.R.: Why do you come up here to do an interview with a magazine that calls itself a Jazz magazine?

B.D.: Well, since you call yourself a review of Jazz and Blues I have to say to myself how much can I say, or how much in depth, and this is very agonizing because one can contradict oneself. If a work of mine is reviewed in a periodical which devotes itself to what is called Jazz music, does that negate my work? If those are the people that are interested in my work, or if because I'm a Black musician that is that title that's assigned to my work, what do I do? Do I come to your office and blow your place up? Well, to get back to the whys of doing an interview like this, and of course my entire life is a contradiction, I'm doing it because I want to do it. That's why I'm doing it. I couldn't be forced to do it. I'm doing it also because I would like certain things to be clarified and I hope that if people are going to deal with what I'm saying I want it to be clear. But, there are certain things I can't control; in the instance of speaking to *Cadence Magazine,* I made a choice. And in that instance, I have the option then of saying what I want to say about myself if anyone is interested in hearing it presented to them. I'm not a Jazz musician, I used to be one, and I was very, very proud to be one, but I also used to be a Negro, I also used to go to the barber every other week because my hair grows fast and I used to keep it at the proper length so that it didn't show itself up as being kinky, you understand. I don't need to do that any more because I reserve the right to develop and get to know myself and to change. I'm a Black man, I'm not an African, I'm not a Arab. I know where I come from, I do *American* music from the perspective of things that effect my life. I'm Black, I'm not White.

R.D.R.: It's still improvised music.

B.D.: Let's say *all* music is improvised.

R.D.R.: I don't think this sort of thing is ever going to be resolved, I think it gets to the personal things. I don't think when I use the word Jazz that I'm being insensitive, because in my mind it is a great compliment.

B.D.: And that isn't even a criticism. Let's say I teach, Bob, and I have to tell people, and I make it as clear as I can, the terms which will be appropriate will be used... Jazz has to be used as does Swing, traditional or Dixieland to make the points. I think a man is a damn fool to think that because he has been emancipated, everything then hinges upon how you do things in terms of the perspective of today. One can use any terms, therefore. Someone will say to me, "Well, what kind of music do you do?" Well, it's very difficult, for you to say something without you seeming to be pretentious, you don't want to tell people actually what you do because it takes too long and it's boring and pretentious. I would like to say *I do music that I think is of incredible interest to me that I feel very strongly about*. But they start turning away immediately. No one wants a heavy conversation from you when they ask you what you do, they want you to say well, I'm a Blues player; I'm a composer;

I'm an arranger, etc. There is such a thing as a Jazz feel, no matter how laborious it is for me to utter that word, (because I have a hostility towards it). But, for want of a better definition, there is a Jazz feel to every area of significant music. I have listened to pieces of, and this is what makes most of my contemporaries either sneer derisively at, or try to say here goes Bill again, I have heard performances of the Vivaldi pieces where there was a Jazz feel from the standpoint of what was being projected. Black people in America are not totally responsible for making 4/4 an important definition of how time is subdivided. And when you tell people when everyone tells you about the significance of a 12-bar Blues and you can tell them that there are some Elizabethan songs that have the form of I, IV, V, I, they look at you with an incredible look. One has to decide if the form is more important than the inflection, and we know there are very, very limited forms that become easily accessible. Once you recognized that no matter what goes down, there has got to be as many ways of looking at that thing or dealing with it as there are people on the face of this earth who are willing to get the relevant kind of experience and background and allow themselves to experience certain things, we don't have a problem.

R.D.R.: Do you have any major regrets in the way you've chosen or taken your life?

B.D.: Absolutely not, no. If I had my life to live over again, I would probably do everything exactly the way I had done it from the standpoint of about 90%. 90% of what, I would do exactly the way I've done it, knowing what I know now.

R.D.R.: And also not knowing what was going to happen.

B.D.: That's right.

R.D.R.: What do you feel have been major triumphs?

B.D.: Staying alive, that's the major one, not going crazy, not having to shoot shit into my arm. Not having to have one monkey on your back which is society, and then putting another motherfucker up there on my back which would be shooting shit in your arm. When I lived in Harlem, there were gangs and I never belonged to a gang. And I never had my ass kicked by any of those people either. I didn't do anything to be one of the boys. I was always an individual. I have never been a good follower. I could never do anything to hurt or disgrace my family anyway, because my stepfather wouldn't have liked it and would probably have killed me. Besides, I loved my mother too much to make her ashamed of me. I could never have gotten into trouble.

When I looked around me and I saw as a very young person what was accessible to me, I made up my mind very, very early what it was I wanted to do and what it was I was not going to do. I was taught very, very candidly, one should not affect any studies in architecture, there were no Black architects. When I said I wanted to be a painter, I was advised to try commercial art. When people talked about going into drama we were cautioned very severely. In fact, actually I was on my way after junior high school, and you're the first person hearing this, to being an auto mechanic because that's what you did with young Black men, you could learn to fix cars. Some teachers of mine became alarmed and informed my parents that this would not be a very wise decision for me because I had certain gifts. So instead of me going then to New York Vocational to learn to be an auto mechanic, which maybe was the wrong decision because at least then I would be able to fix my own goddamn car, I went off to study art and painting, another direction. Because even then there were certain people who recognized that conceivably there were certain other things that I could do.

R.D.R.: Where did you go to high school?

B.D.: To Commerce High School, which had then one of the best art departments. It's now Brandeis High School, down at Lincoln Center; that's where I spent my high school years. Of my seven classes everyday, three of them were in art, that's how gifted I was. When I was 14, I had already been studying, privately painting ever since I was nine years old.

R.D.R.: It's surprising to me what I've read that you ever did get into music, because your talent is obviously strong enough in art and the training was there.

B.D.: It's all in the same variable. Painting you can only see and you can't see music.

R.D.R.: What did your stepfather do?

B.D.: He worked as a laborer, but he was a mathematician by training. And a professional athlete.

R.D.R.: And your mother, I read, was an artist and a Blues singer. Not a recorded Blues singer, right?

B.D.: Yes. Sang Blues around the house till it was revolting.

R.D.R.: You never mentioned your father. He was out of the picture.

B.D.: No, I never knew him.

R.D.R.: How old is your mother?

B.D.: I'm 55. I was born when my mother was 18 years old. She's 73. She lives in the Bronx (N.Y.), with my two sisters and younger brother.

R.D.R.: Often when you are referred to in the media it's in conjunction with your early work with Mr. Shepp.

B.D.: He and I worked together, which was very positive. Archie Shepp, however, was allowed to extend his career. In certain ways, mine was both truncated, and broadened. People think of my work as having ended (if for them it did exist at all) because of the extensive public work that he went on to do. All the recordings; the notoriety, etc.... The thing was, for me, how does one resolve the fact that I don't think of music as being an olympics situation? I just don't believe that. If you wanted to say, "Who could hold a note on a horn without taking a breath and without doing circular breathing?", then that's olympics. I'll tell you where I'm experiencing incredible difficulties sometimes;

the fact that I have to be very dispassionate when I teach courses. We have a very basic course, the introduction to Black music, which is a survey course—I can't really speak about those people the way I sometimes feel about those people. I have to deal with their contributions. Sometimes it becomes very, very difficult.

R.D.R.: Do you speak with Shepp? Are you on terms with him now?

B.D.: No, Archie did some things to make it so I don't find it necessary to have any kind of relationship with him.

R.D.R.: Does this have roots back at the Jazz Guild and Impulse Records?

B.D.: Long before that. Oh, yes, there was a thing that happened about Impulse Records. The thing about it was, when Archie Shepp and I first recorded and wanted to lease that first record, no one wanted it. That record, the first Savoy one, the one I get no money for, no one wanted that recording, and Savoy Records was the last recording company on the list of all the recording companies in this country that I had canvassed. And when that record was done, it was leased to Savoy for one dollar, and before you know it, Archie Shepp became a hero; because of his friends. From then on Archie Shepp went on to various kinds of things based on that initiation, not because of his work with Cecil Taylor. Shepp speaks eloquently about how much he learned from Taylor, but I seriously doubt if he really learned anything at all. Shepp was quite a pressing person about wanting to get somewhere—and where is there to go?—and for this he was fired by Taylor for playing too goddamn long in an instance at the Five Spot when Taylor wanted to cut things short. My initial attraction to Archie was because he was a playwright in addition to being a musician and had other interests. I don't really have that much of an affinity for most musicians simply because they are much too monochromatic. But then in recent years I've had to tell myself, and thus realize, that one cannot stay in a room learning to play an instrument literally all of your life and then be expected to know anything else. Archie had an alert mind; rehearsals were a pleasure; we started to work together and that was it. A lot of dues were paid for that but a lot of good and interesting music and musical situations evolved. Archie, however, immediately marshaled his forces. Recently, much to my surprise, he did acknowledge in print that I was the one that advised him to speak to John Coltrane about possibly helping him get a record date for the Impulse label. And prior to Shepp's becoming a rather "valuable artistic force" for Impulse neither Bob Thiele nor anyone else of the record moguls would speak to me or Shepp. It's amazing how soon people forget where they once were. But we did discuss his speaking to John Coltrane, who was then recording with regularity for Impulse. At the time, all of these musicians were using Coltrane. Trane was probably, of all the significant musicians, the most sensitive and the most kind. It seemed to me that no matter what they did he could manage to see and hear some significant musicological point trying to be expressed or at least being in existence. A lot of those people I don't think dug him at all; they saw themselves as getting somewhere so they would, irrespective of their musical qualifications at the time, sit in with him. I know that to some of those musicians sitting in with Trane had little to do with their even attempting to understand why he was allowing them on that bandstand anyway. They were more concerned with doing their own individual thing, if it could be called that. And it must have literally drove the regular members of the band up the wall.

But John's music and direction had such an inner strength to it that his musical point of view could sustain what was or wasn't happening. To my way of thinking he represented the epitome of being an art musician. Very strong with the relevant amount of sensitivity and compassion. And if you want to really understand that, listen to the Ascension album where none of them understood why John Coltrane had them there. As a classic of the New Music it sustains the theory that the cream does finally come to the top.

R.D.R.: Freddie Hubbard admitted that. (See the Freddie Hubbard interview.)

B.D.: Yes, well Freddie was honest about it. But in spite of the attitudes of the others, music emerged. From 1962—1963 I was unable to play. I ruined my embouchure by trying to change it, and since I was unable to perform I concentrated mainly on writing, practicing, and technical studies to help me get my chops back. Shortly after I'd returned from the Scandinavian tour in 1962, Shepp and John Tchicai had started to work together—and they did sound good—and the New York Contemporary Five was formed with Don Cherry taking my place in the group that had formerly been the Archie Shepp-Bill Dixon Quartet which, when in New York, we had used Tchicai. And because I did need money to pay for my studies and also because neither Shepp nor Tchicai could, Tchicai commissioned me to write the library for the group. When Shepp finally got to do the thing for Impulse, much later, since at that time I was very much aware of how fickle a public could be (if you're out or off the so-called scene then you must be dead), he and I had an oral agreement that when he did the recording, I would do the writing. Mr. Shepp violated that situation. He decided to do the writing himself; and the writing was good because Archie is a good writer and the one piece that he didn't do he had Roswell Rudd do. Archie Shepp and I had formerly shared many an hour together lamenting the dilemma that both of us had when Thiele wouldn't spit on either of us, so it did seem strange or odd at the time, as it does now, that when he was finally ensconced with Impulse, never once, to my knowledge (and he knew that I needed a record) did he attempt to do for me that which he had convinced John Coltrane to do for him.

R.D.R.: How long have you known Cecil Taylor?

B.D.: I have known Taylor since 1951. We met at a session in Harlem at a place called the Sportsmen's Club; a private club that had its own membership. There was a small bar; a bandstand and a dance floor. Young people used to come there to socialize, dance and listen to the music. On Thursday nights the place was open for Jazz music and it was an opportunity for younger musicians to get a chance to both play and meet other musicians. The club was located on the basement level right next door to the Roosevelt Theatre on 145th Street and Seventh Avenue. There were lots of musicians that would come there on those Thursday nights; Tina Brooks, Minor Robinson, Sid McKay, Buckey Thorpe, Floyed Benny (né Bernard Floyd)—Benny was a rather interesting player that has his name misspelled in Valerie Wilmer's book as Benning, and I was the one that went to Alaska with him in a show band that also included alto saxophonist Howard Johnson who had been in the Dizzy Gillespie Big Band... but, excuse me I'm digressing. Yes, I met Taylor in 1951 and he and I have shared many, many interesting moments together intellectually, socially, and naturally musically. We have done a lot of playing together. In fact, when he first was going to Boston to do the first recorded thing that he did on the old Transition label he and I discussed it rather thoroughly and he wanted me to come to Boston with him as a sort of what you might call a "musical support" figure; but I was unable to take the time off from my job at the United Nations. When he first became involved with the first recording for Blue Note, Unit Structures, he and I discussed all of the ramifications of that at my place on Bank Street, in fact the photograph that is used on the cover of one of his Arista records was taken in my place by Ray Ross after a dinner there. In those days we used to do a lot of talking about the so-called future of this music; how could we get the music into the college and university structure along with some of the people who actually did the music being among some of its teachers? In 1958, when I convened the first panel discussion in the United Nations Secretariat building under the auspices of the United Nations Jazz Society of which I was then the president, Cecil Taylor was invited, and played his newly acquired test recording of his later to be released album on Contemporary, "Looking Ahead: The Cecil Taylor Quartet," along with George Russell, Gunther Schuller, Martin Williams (subbing for Nat Hentoff), Carl Bowman, a former teacher of composition of mine who, years later, was to appear on John Coltrane's "Africa Brass" album, with Jimmie Giuffre and vibist Earl Griffith in the audience. After the October Revolution Series was completed it was Cecil Taylor and I who initiated the first discussions on the then viability of collectivizing ourselves (all of us musicians who were then not working) and engaging in the struggles of both body and soul survival and spiritual, intellectual and artistic survival. Taylor and I have been through a lot together and there have been those times when I've not seen or spoken to him for years. We have had our share of disagreements. But I do call him and he does stay in touch with me. In fact, of all the musicians that were engaged in the artistically bankrupt and financially losing fiasco called Bennington Summers that some people from my own school mounted in 1976, the year I went to Vienna and did the recording with Franz Kogelmann—of all the musicians who were contracted and consulted to do this "Jazz" version of *Gone With the Wind* , only Cecil Taylor had the tenacity, decency and integrity to call and ask me what the situation really was about and why I wasn't lending my name and the support of my own department to the venture. The rest of these "Jazz" musicians acted as though they didn't know that I was there; that there obviously must have been something wrong that I disagreed with from the standpoints of ethics, aesthetics and social philosophy. But Taylor called both to inquire as to my position and for information. You will note that he did not participate in that venture. Whenever I've wanted or needed to make musical use of any members of Taylor's Unit—I've used Alan Silva in my work and also had him as a Visiting Artist here and in 1975 when I went on a sabbatical leave I recruited Jimmy Lyons to take my place—I've always checked and cleared it with Taylor first, as a matter of both courtesy and respect. I knew Taylor when he was a dishwasher, when he served in the capacity of a "delivery boy"; I worked in an area, as a shipping clerk, where he once had a job delivering lunches in the Madison Avenue advertising district and on my lunch hour I would go with him on his "rounds" so that we could continue our discussions of things that we both felt were rather important in terms of the plight of the Black artist in America. I found it rather distressing that some things that were recently attributed to me as saying about him in print, taken out of context, naturally, were relayed to him by some people that have had mutual contact, musically, with the both of us. But you want to know something? In the many, many interviews that have been granted to Cecil Taylor, to my knowledge, he has never once mentioned my name. Don't you find that interesting?

R.D.R.: I find it surprising. Well, I suspect that Cecil Taylor then hasn't been asked directly about certain...

B.D.: Everyone of a certain persuasion has been asked directly about me. It's impossible to not deal with me, relating to a certain time, place, and events.

R.D.R.: I know in the interviews we have done in *Cadence*, you have come up quite often.

B.D.: True, I have to come up.

R.D.R.: Well, evidently you don't have to come up.

B.D.: Well, I have to come up, but I don't obviously have to do any more than come up. I remember Thelonious Monk during the height of the Bebop movement, when Herbie Nichols wrote the first article on him because Monk, at that time, didn't even fit in with that movement, as radical as the boppers were. They didn't know what to do with Thelonious Monk. Now mind you, I'm not placing myself in that category; I'm just saying that there are some people that no one knows what the fuck to do with. How many cats do you find who play like Thelonious Monk and how many cats do you find that play like Bud Powell? Who had the most "accessible" idea and element to be both "understood" and then subsequently available for parceling out to the scavengers?

R.D.R.: Bud Powell.

B.D.: And this isn't being said to in any way denigrate the awesome genius of Powell. I am only trying to make a point that obviously I should have known from past experiences is impossible to make simple, because the powers that be have systematically drummed into one's detractors that all they have to do is detract; not think of what is being presented to them as a body of possible usable information, just detract.

But everyone knows that it took Monk years before they would even begin to discuss him at all. He was far too radical in almost everything that he did and was for the boppers and their supporters. Didn't Andre Previn once say that Monk shouldn't be allowed to touch a piano as a player? How many years was it before so-called Jazz musicians from the new music of the '40s would take the time to even learn his pieces of music? Wasn't his music called "too difficult"?

R.D.R.: I don't think what you say, though, invalidates all or even the majority of Archie Shepp's work.

B.D.: Well, I wouldn't, simply because it would be presumptuous of me and too time consuming from my own work efforts, to sit in judgment of Shepp's work. I mean, the people who pay him to make those recordings and who consequently support him, that's their responsibility. All I can say, for whatever it is worth to anyone that would feel it necessary to ask me the question, if he's finally both discovered and "absorbed" Duke Ellington, that is his problem. I mean, hell, I prefer to hear Ben Webster. I don't need anyone to paraphrase Ben Webster to let me know how great that shit is.

R.D.R.: And the funny thing is, he says the same thing about Scott Hamilton.

B.D.: Yes, because its easy to talk about the failings or levels of parasitism of the White musician. We live in a society where the omnipresent THEY allows you to do whatever you do, even if you're not doing it at the level of your social pronouncements. Personally for me, Mr. Shepp's work, when he didn't "know as much" and hadn't been touted as much, was much more direct and honest simply because he could then only play who he was.

R.D.R.: I think that's true.

B.D.: Listen, I'm not saying that he's not a damn good player. I think his "Four for Trane" is a gem; the things that he did with the two trombones and bass and drums demonstrate a sensitivity and musical awareness that few of his contemporaries on the instrument even dreamed was possible; and his version of

Johnny Mandel's "The Shadow of Your Smile," which, for the Live at Doneschingen album he retitles as a Homage to Trane, is a beautiful work and I'm sure that I've missed some of the other more stable and enduring efforts that he has made, but Archie has been PAID to learn how to "play" and I'm defining this being able to "play" within the framework of the definition prevalent among the majority of "listeners" to the music. And, to a degree, that's fine. Why shouldn't one continuously "develop" and at the same time be paid and rewarded for it? But, let's face it, if his (Shepp's) discovery of the Dizzy Gillespie Big Band and those kinds of voicings and textures, and Duke Ellington are as "revolutionary," as dogma, as that, then it must have been as *revolutionary as a bitch* for the people who knew and recognized the importance and significance of the music *before* others like him discovered it!! Too much, in my opinion, has been made about so-called, or former "avant-garde" musicians from the '60s, and their all-of-a-sudden "discovery" of the traditional, to this music, song forms and the ramifications of their now new-found ability to use traditional harmony and forms in a matrix situation with their now more "contemporary," they please their "critics," approaches to music. Of course we know that the *important* thing is to "communicate" with a wider audience because this almost automatically is thought to provide one with a better mode of living. Again, I have to reiterate, this is just one man's opinion.

R.D.R.: Suddenly this whole thing starts to seem divisive.

B.D.: Why does the truth as *I* seem to see it, based on my experiences and what have you, "suddenly" become divisive?? Try to look at it this way, Archie Shepp and I are both considered professors of music; I'm tenured and I would imagine that he is also, the epitome of a hierarchy to be reached by Black "Jazz" musicians according to a telephone conversation that I had with a *Downbeat* editor, and we're both musicians. However, in relation to this, one of us teaches and heads a department and has also researched, devised and written a curriculum that is in usage for his department—me; the other one, Shepp, hasn't. Now how can he, in spite of not being able to, be both of these things? I don't claim to do what he does; I don't claim to be as "important" or as "significant" as he is. For whatever reason, I don't have 100 recordings commercially available; I don't for whatever reason, continuously tour all over the world; I'm not, for whatever reason, interviewed all the time thus being allowed to voice my concerns about the "injustices" seemingly endemic to America. Archie Shepp and I are obviously different, so why is it again conveniently construed as being "divisive" if I feel that it has to be articulated, *especially,* if once every millennium I'm given the opportunity to respond to something that obviously I must feel rather strong about? Why is it, among all the things almost constantly under discussion in this genre of world music, that no one wants to discuss this?? Why does it make people uncomfortable to hear that, among the musicians in this area of music, that there are *differences* among these musicians, both in terms of lifestyle, aims and feelings concerning how those aims might conceivably be achieved? Why must we, very hypocritically, affect being a mutual admiration society, especially when that is certainly *not* the case? You want to know something? It is my opinion that this entire situation concerning so-called "divisiveness," being "angry" and "hostile" reflects more what interviews are doing for people who want to hear what the people being interviewed are doing and how *only* if that *doesn't* bring along with it too much information that might not be considered popular. In other words; tell, and give, the people what they want and *then* let everybody retire to their own small enclaves laying the blame on the "theys" for the lack of a sufficient assault on the real problem by the, theoretically at least, most aggrieved. Right?

The angriest man anyone ever knew was Louis Armstrong singing. I had to tell Archie that one time. I said, "How in the fuck are you gonna be angry?" Listen to him sing "Hello Dolly," now there's some anger there. Because he knew how he got to where he was and how long he was gonna be here, 'cause they didn't really *dig* his trumpet playing. I said to Archie once, "You think you're angry, 'cause you're always starting up at the mouth. How do you feel a man like Louis felt knowing he's gonna die?"

And how he got to where he was not because of his playing, because of his tomming. But like, he came from another generation. The only time Louis ever spoke out about anything, even when he was made king of the Zulus. In New Orleans there were certain hotels he couldn't stay in, he never said anything. Once Louis said something, something that got so bad he had to say something.

R.D.R.: The Little Rock (Arkansas) desegregation situation during the Eisenhower administration.

B.D.: That's right. I said to Archie, "So here you are a college graduate, someone else has gone through all the fuckin' lynching, through all the wars, through all this shit, you come on out, you go on welfare 'cause you got married and had a couple of kids and *you're* angry. What the fuck are you talking about? I come from a different generation."

R.D.R.: That's right. But, that is part of it, Bill, you do.

B.D.: I'm glad I come from that generation. That's one of the only saving graces, as visibly annoyed as I am about certain things. I'm not like them. They want too much and they don't want to give a shit.

R.D.R.: But, you know, it's true of a lot of people, whether or not it's true of Archie Shepp.

B.D.: That's no excuse for their behavior. They want everything, forgetting that everyone is always wanting everything. See, because if you owe someone something you take care of your obligation. Well, that's what a lot of these people do. They take everything they can get, then *they* bitch. A guy comes to you, he says, "Lend me $10." You say, "Fine." Next week he comes to you, "Lend me $50." "Fine." He comes six months later and says, "I need $100." You say, "Fine." You never ask him for the money. And he starts hating you because you're in the position to lend him the fuckin' money. You're only doing what the man is asking, then the next thing you know he goes to see his analyst and tells you, "Yeah man, I became too dependent upon you," and begins to hate you. What is this bullshit—some of us resent it. So the next time a guy come up to you and says give me $5, say, *"Go get a job!"*(laughter). I mean is that what you're supposed to do? A guy comes up to you, he says, "Give me $.50 for a bottle of wine." You say, "I'll give you $.50 if you'll get a bottle of soup." Is that what you're suppose to do?

R.D.R.: I don't think there is any hard and fast way to approach that thing.

B.D.: No, but the best thing is a guy says, "Gimme $.50," you say as eloquently and with as much diction as you can muster, "I don't speak English," and then walk off (laughter).

EDITOR'S NOTE: *We began talking about age.*

B.D.: Forty was the dividing line. You were then neither a young man, nor an old man. And I can remember thinking, "Oh, my god," but it was really funny when I became 40, I became fully awake and when I was getting towards 50 I said, "Oh, my god, I'm going to be half a century old!" (laughter). Then, I'm now what you would call middle aged! (laughter). The only problem with me is I have no sense of age at all, I don't have one. I had a marvelous thing happen to me, I lost a year last year. When my birthday came I thought I was going to be 56, I was only 55! (laughter). Now I'm going to be 56 again. I'm going to be four years from 60 (laughter). But you know what it does to you, it lets you know how fragile you are and at the same time just how much you had better be taking care of a certain amount of business.

R.D.R.: Well, it gives you a greater sense of resolve.

B.D.: Really. And you get over those things. Now what I seem to see with so many of the people that I've discussed in certain kinds of ways: they have no sense that there is an ultimate someplace and that they will be accountable at some point. In other words, their records may die with them, or die before they do. The fact is that you don't just take from a society, you give something. And your giving doesn't just happen to be because you were born.

R.D.R.: Who do you feel still has integrity?

B.D.: Integrity—you make me feel like a pompous ass. In my opinion, a person I can listen to and hear a lot of music and serious intent is Cecil Taylor; he does what he does with such definition. And when Miles Davis *plays* I still hear some things. I'm not saying when the band plays, but when he plays.

R.D.R.: You told me earlier that years ago when you got rid of your first record collection that you kept 50 records. What are some of the improvised (Jazz) music ones?

B.D.: I had "Piano Reflections," solo piano by Ellington, a considerable amount of Miles Davis, Cecil Taylor. Some Charlie Parker, John Coltrane, some piano pieces by Bud Powell, Herbie Nichols, Thelonious Monk.

R.D.R.: Which Monk, "Five by Five"?

B.D.: Yes, I especially like that and some piano solos. There was George Russell's "Jazz in the Space Age." They were things that I knew every time I listened I knew I would be drawn to. And there was Ornette on tenor. And Sonny Rollins' "Our Man in Jazz."

R.D.R.: It's a shame that by surviving, artists seem to have to destroy themselves.

B.D.: It's like a two-edged sword. How do you win?

R.D.R.: Make a pact with the devil and die at 35.

B.D.: Or, know when you shouldn't be playing things simply to be playing things.

R.D.R.: Or don't release them.

B.D.: Right. Or be like Horowitz if one could. Horowitz decided he couldn't play because he was too nervous to perform in public. He stopped playing.

R.D.R.: It's presumptuous for me to speak for Sonny Rollins, but it seems to me that it was a decision he could have made, he could afford to say okay I will only release one record every three years now.

B.D.: I would say that, and you would say that too, and I've known a great many people that could've said that, but they don't. They continue to release as many records as they can. I don't know who made the proposition, I read it years ago, there was something said about the best way to insure for both the listening public, the best quality, and therefore to insure that records would be purchased by interested listeners. And to insure also that the artist was able to do things he really wanted and from the standpoint of posterity, would be for a person to record at various times during the year. Or when things seemed to be right. And then just leave those and then maybe two or three years later go through them and see what seems to have held up. If you could educate musicians to the fact that this is posterity they're dealing with. This is like your children. You don't want to have a child with six fingers, or three knees. But, a lot of records have six fingers and three knees, because the people have made no effort to see that that doesn't happen.

R.D.R.: And that's more true today than ever before.

B.D.: And, you have a legacy of good improvising, a history of what has happened because we *do* have records; we can listen, we can study. For example, it seems to me we are now having to deal with composition, or the organization of something, much more so than we had to do before. We can't trust this improviser, not on his own.

EDITOR'S NOTE: *The rest becomes far too personal for public consumption at this particular point in history.*

R.D.R.: How did you come upon your job teaching at Bennington College?

B.D.: I was asked, along with the dancer-choreographer Judith Dunn, to come there two years in a row, which, because of previous professional commitments in New York and elsewhere, I was at first unable to do. One year I was unable because during that summer I was a composer in residence at George Washington University in Washington, D.C., and during the other part of the year I was directing the music program of the University of the Streets, program that I had formulated and started. In 1968 I was free from both those commitments, I was fired from the University of the Streets because it was finally felt by the Puerto Ricans that ran the place that my music approach to both teaching and aesthetics—the music, they felt, didn't sufficiently relate to the people in the streets—was inappropriate for that setting. I was replaced at the University of the Streets by the late Kenny Dorham; he was then attending New York University trying to finish his undergraduate degree—unfortunately allowed them to persuade him to bring an ersatz Rock and Roll situation there, which they soon became disenchanted with; and then they hired Jackie McLean, who was then, if memory serves me correctly, replaced by the pianist Andrew Hill. Free from that situation I then in 1968 accepted a part-time teaching assignment in the Dance Division of Bennington College where Judith Dunn and I taught collectively composition for musicians, dancers, composers and choreographers. She taught technique classes for dancers and I played the piano for those classes. We also taught, collaboratively, beginning dance composition. I also worked, when I became full time, 1969, in the regular music department there. In 1971, I took a year's leave from Bennington and became a Visiting Professor in the School of Music at the University of Wisconsin. I loved it out there. It was through Cecil Taylor, who had been an Artist in Residence there the previous year, and who in 1971 went on to a better artistic situation for himself at Antioch College in Yellowsprings, that I secured this position as he alerted the Search Committee to my work and experience in that area of academic work. Before I went to Bennington I was also teaching at Columbia University Teachers' College in dance with Miss Dunn.

At this point, the conversation was interrupted by a phone call from a musician who had submitted tapes of his music to Cadence Jazz Records for proposed release on that label. When Bob Rusch, in the capacity of producer, did not concur with the musician about his assessment of the music, the conversation became unpleasant and heated.

R.D.R.: (Referring to the phone call) If that man could get me as worked up over his music as he did on the phone, we'd be releasing it!

B.D.: You cannot have a situation where these musicians coming from a background where they have, in return for free labor, all of their needs were met: housing, clothing, all those things, called welfare today. In other words, those people then never had to do anything except work. That is still a part of the consciousness of these people. The way they look at you is as a man who has to get $100,000, open a club and give them work. Or form a record company and make records for them. Or to open a booking agency and get them jobs. What happens is the musicians today become very, very confused about their roles, and the ones they would really like to talk that way to is, say, the head of Columbia, Victor, Arista. Those guys however, won't even spit on them; the records won't even get past the secretary. This is called biting the hand that feeds you, the person who they have entrée to, the person they can speak to directly on the phone they wreak their venom on them and try to turn you around. That kind of conversation is classic. It's fine. You said to him (telephone call) something that was very interesting, "You have one record out. If that one that you have out is so great, why aren't you dealing with those other people for this one?" It's a sad situation.

R.D.R.: Well he was trying to tell me both what an artistic success it was and what a commercial success it is.

B.D.: Well, because they know how to take advantage.

R.D.R.: Well, if you balance it out I think there is no doubt that it is the artist who gets most taken advantage of—Columbia Records did not build Black music, Black music built Columbia Records.

B.D.: Well, the system works in a certain way, but you've gotta remember that we are all a part of this system. It takes two to tango, two people moving in a certain kind of way. My consternation was years ago when I was really interested in some of these things, I would talk to these people (artists) about what conceivably they could learn how to do if they were to become responsible. They would always make a very offensive statement to me, they would say man, you're talking like a White man, as if being able to see a problem, sift it through your mind and then decide on a course of what might be positive action—positive to you and *your* future well being and health—was solely and only indigenous to the White race. Just like musicians bragging, and not too many years ago, that all they wanted to do was "swing," suggesting that any awareness concerning your *daily* plight in life as a human being could only be indicative of your being less of a *talented*—and thus deserving of further recognition, by the powers that be—so-called Jazz musician than the rest. Yes, I have had several very well-known musicians, in effect, say that to me, to which I've had to say, "You don't have to worry about me speaking to you at all." In other words, they were able to translate, "Well we do it this way, and they do it that way." But you're coming to them.

R.D.R.: And you always will be as long as you do that.

B.D.: You better believe it.

Discography

The following listing of records offers fine examples of each individual's art. I have only listed albums on which the individual under discussion is the leader and only those records which are among the best of what is available. All the records were available as of January 1984. However, because the currency of the Jazz catalogue is always changing, and because distribution of Jazz recordings is poor throughout the world, they may not be easily attainable. There are numerous mail-order houses which specialize in Jazz products. One of the best is Northcountry Record Distributors, 345 Rt. 1, Redwood, New York 13679.

Freddie Hubbard

Not all Freddie Hubbard records are of equal quality. Some of his finest work on Blue Note and Impulse records is no longer available and much of what is available and current is of little interest to the listener of creative improvised music.

First Light / CTI 6013: This record perhaps captures creative energy in a somewhat commercial setting better than any other Hubbard recording. Also notable on this recording is the outstanding guitar work by George Benson.

Freddie Hubbard Live / Pablo 2620 113: Recorded in 1980, almost ten years after the *First Light* date, it is almost an updated overview of his earlier work.

Outpost / Enja 3095: This is perhaps the most straight ahead and finest example of Mr. Hubbard's work since his move away from commercialism.

PAUL QUINICHETTE

There are not still available many records led by Paul Quinichette. Most are now out of print.

On the Sunny Side / Original Jazz Classics OJC-076: This is a 1957 jamming date with Quinichette leading a sextet.

Prevue / Famous Door HL-106: A 1974 quartet recording with pianist Brooks Kerr as co-leader.

Kansas City Joys / Sonet 716 (Sweden): A 1976 date with Mr. Quinichette comfortable in a group which included tenor sax man Buddy Tate, pianist Jay McShann, and violinist Claude Williams.

Milt Jackson

Milt Jackson has recorded prolifically and in the company of almost all of the finest Jazz men of the Bop era. Most of his numerous recordings as a member of the Modern Jazz Quartet are no longer available; however, most currently available Milt Jackson recordings are of good quality.

The Modern Jazz Quartet, *Concorde* / Original Jazz Classics - 002: This is an early and excellent example of the Modern Jazz Quartet from the mid-'50s.

Ain't But a Few of Us Left / Pablo 2310-873, recorded almost 30 years after the *Concorde* date, uses the same quartet format, but this time with Oscar Peterson on piano, bassist Ray Brown, and drummer Grady Tate—an outstanding example of Mr. Jackson's soulful playing.

Cecil Taylor

Since he was rarely recorded in the '50s, and '60s, most of Mr. Taylor's early records are now unavailable.

Looking Ahead / Contemporary S7562: This is a 1958 recording, one of the few early recordings of Cecil Taylor still available. It's interesting as a precursor of things to come and an indication of some of the sources of Cecil Taylor music.

Dark to Themselves / Enja 2084 (West Germany): Two side-long improvisations make up this live 1976 recording which also features the sax playing of Jimmy Lyons and David Ware along with Raphe Malik on trumpet, and Marc Edwards on drums.

Three Phasis / New World NW303: This 1978 piece runs over 57 minutes and is packed with power and discovery rarely matched.

One Too Many Salty Swift and Not Goodbye / hat Hut HH 3R02: This is a three record set that presents almost 2¼ hours of improvisation which will both exhilarate and exhaust the listener—a great display of both the mental and physical stamina of Cecil Taylor.

Sun Ra

Sun Ra has released a tremendous number of records on his own label, El Saturn, and other associated labels. These records are often of an inferior quality, are irregularly available, but overall offer the most complete chronology of Mr. Ra's work of the past 30 years.

Live at Montreux / Inner City IC-1039.

Sunrise in Different Dimensions / hat Hut 2R17.

Both of these records display the Sun Ra Arkestra at its best. The Montreux set is from 1976, the hat Hut from 1980. Both issues are two-record sets and demonstrate Mr. Ra's gifts in programs which combine Jazz standards and Ra originals.

Milt Hinton

Ironically, although bassist Milt Hinton has probably appeared on more different Jazz sessions as a sideman than any other artist, he has been the leader on only four LP dates. His *Here Swings the Judge* on Famous Door (HL 104) combines a tender 1964 duo date with the great tenor saxist Ben Webster (who also bangs out some stride piano here), and a swinging 1975 sextet date which included trumpeter Jon Faddis and sax men Frank Wess and Budd Johnson.

Von Freeman

Von Freeman has recorded only a handful of recordings since the beginning of his professional career in the early '50s. Fortunately, his three finest releases to date are all available. They are all quartet dates using his Chicago based rhythm section of David Shipp (bassist), Charles Walton or Wilbur Campbell (drummer) and the very underrated pianist John Young. The records were all recorded in the mid-'70s and present a program mostly of standards played in extended performance.

Have No Fear / Nessa N-8.

Serenade & Blues / Nessa-11.

Young and Foolish / Daybreak D-002 (Netherlands).

Billy Harper

While Billy Harper has recorded almost a dozen records as leader, none of them is readily available in the United States as a domestic issue. All of his recordings are of a high standard. Of his recordings still in print the Italian issues are easiest to find, but his finest efforts are on the Japanese releases.

Knowledge of Self / Denon YX 7801-ND (Japanese): A quintet date from 1978, this is my favorite Harper recording and one of the great recordings of the '70s. The program is made up of two original compositions, each taking up an entire side of the record.

Soran-Bushi, B.H. / Denon YX 7522-ND (Japanese).

Live on the Sudan / Denon YZ-138-ND (Japanese).

The Believer / Baystate RVJ 6083 (Japanese).

On Tour in Europe / Black Saint BSR 0001 (Italian).

In Europe / Soul Note SN 1001 (Italian).

Art Blakey

Art Blakey has recorded over 100 LPs. Very few of them are less than good. At any one time there are usually at least two dozen Blakey LPs in catalogue.

A Night at Birdland Volume One and *Two* / Blue Note 1521 and 1522 (Japanese): These are 1954 live recordings of the first great Jazz Messenger group (Clifford Brown, trumpet; Lou Donaldson, alto sax; Horace Silver, piano; Curly Russell, bass). They are two of the most exciting and vibrant recordings in modern Jazz history.

Hard Bop / Columbia Jazz Odyssey PC 36809: The 1956 edition of the Jazz Messengers, this included Jackie McLean on alto sax and Bill Hardman on trumpet.

Caravan / Original Jazz Classics OJC-038: This early '60s edition of the Messengers included Freddie Hubbard's trumpet, Wayne Shorter's tenor sax, Curtis Fuller on trombone, and pianist Cedar Walton.

Album of the Year / Timeless SJP 155 (Holland): The 1981 Messengers present trumpeter Wynton Marsalis, sax men Robert Watson and Billy Pierce, plus James Williams's piano and Charles Fambrough, bass.

Keystone 3 / Concord CJ-196: The 1982 Messengers live in San Francisco with Marsalis, Pierce and Fambrough, plus Don Brown (piano) and Branford Marsalis (alto sax).

Jazz Messengers with Thelonious Monk / Atlantic 1278: A 1957 collaboration between the music of Monk, on the date the pianist and composer of five of the six compositions, and the style and drive of Blakey and his Messengers. No other drummer worked quite as well with Monk and his music.

Bill Dixon

Bill Dixon has had very few recordings released. All that have been are of interest, but not easily obtained. After 13 years with no commercially released recordings, Mr. Dixon has allowed five releases since 1980.

Considerations One and *Two* / Fore 3 and 4 (Italian): These two records are recordings made by Bill Dixon between 1972 and 1976. They help fill in the space between his 1967 recording for RCA (*Intents & Purposes*), and recent Soul Note recordings.

Bill Dixon in Italy Volume One and *Two* / Soul Note SN 1008 and SN 1011: 1980 recordings with Arthur Brooks and Stephen Haynes (trumpets), Steve Horenstein (reeds), Freddie Waits (drums) and Alan Silva (bass).

November 1981 / Soul Note SN 1037/38 is a magnificent two record set from 1981. These quartet sides with Alan Silva and Mario Pavone (basses) and Lawrence Cook (drums) are perhaps the most completely realized music by Bill Dixon released to date.

Index

This is a selected index and does not have an entry for every name or place mentioned. It is set up for the researcher as a reference to items given more than just passing reference.